D1230463

AFRO-AMERICAN GENEALOGY SOURCEBOOK

GARLAND REFERENCE LIBRARY
OF SOCIAL SCIENCE
(VOL. 321)

AFRO-AMERICAN GENEALOGY SOURCEBOOK

Tommie Morton Young

GARLAND PUBLISHING, INC. • NEW YORK & LONDON
1987

© 1987 Tommie Morton Young
All rights reserved

Library of Congress Cataloging-in-Publication Data

Young, Tommie M. (Tommie Morton)
Afro-American genealogy sourcebook.

(Garland reference library of social science ; vol 321)
Includes bibliographical references.
1. Afro-Americans—Genealogy—Handbooks, manuals, etc.
2. Afro-Americans—Genealogy—Bibliography.
3. Afro-Americans—Genealogy—Archival resources—
Directories. I. Title. II. Series: Garland reference
library of social science ; v. 321)
E185.96.Y67 1987 929'.1'08996073 85-45112
ISBN 0-8240-8684-8 (alk. paper)

Cover design by Renata Gomes

Printed on acid-free, 250-year-life paper
Manufactured in the United States of America

ACKNOWLEDGMENTS

A special word of thanks must go to the agencies, individuals, and organizations who responded to the surveys and cooperated in the interviews that were initiated in the preparation of this work.

To
African and African-American Families
with special reference to the
Lane and Morton families
of Tennessee

CONTENTS

Preface	ix
Introduction	1
Part I	
BACKGROUND READING AND BASIC REFERENCE SOURCES	4
A. Background Reading	4
B. Basic Reference Sources, Afro-Americana	27
C. Basic Genealogy Reference Sources	35
Part II	
PRIVATE RESOURCES	45
A. Sites and Locations	46
B. Churches	50
C. Cemeteries and Burial Grounds	55
D. Manuscripts	59
E. Bibles	69
F. Photographs	70
G. Societies and Organizations	73
H. Education Institutions - Private	77
I. Miscellaneous Sources	77
Part III	
PUBLIC RECORDS AND RESOURCES	82
A. Federal Records and Resources	83
B. City, County, and State Records	111
Part IV	
DIRECTORY OF RESOURCES	135
A. Sources for Vital Statistics: Births, Deaths, and Marriages	136
B. Public Libraries	144
C. Some Major Collections and Libraries for Genealogy Research	166
D. Historically Black Colleges and Universities	181
E. Some Genealogical and Historical Societies and Organizations	188
F. Key to Location Symbols	195

PREFACE

The *Afro-American Genealogy Sourcebook* identifies types of materials used in Afro-American genealogy research, gives examples of these types, and lists locations of specific and potential research materials. The materials listed are primary and secondary sources. A survey of over two hundred libraries and collections of genealogy and history organizations and societies was undertaken to identify as many resources as possible that have not been considered in other genealogy publications. Many of these resources are included in this work. In addition, the author examined numerous state library and archives collections, special university library collections, and private collections of individuals.

The *Sourcebook* is divided into four parts: Part I, Background Readings and Basic Reference Sources; Part II, Private Resources; Part III, Public Resources, and Part IV, Directory of Resources. Information is presented in outlined sections.

Each part of the *Sourcebook* begins with an Introduction, and many of the sections have brief prefatory remarks. Brief annotations are included for many of the titles included in the work. Quotation marks in each of the annotations indicate a direct quote from the source. Many of the titles are explanatory and as such may not include annotations. Part IV, Directory of Resources, includes the Key to Locations Symbols used in the body of the work.

Afro-American Genealogy Sourcebook

INTRODUCTION

Genealogy is the study of relationships between individuals and of families composed of related individuals.[1] It is also that branch of history which involves the determination of family relationships.[2] A broader view of *genealogy* takes into account family relationships in a wider historical and social context. Work of this kind is called *family history*.[3] The genealogist concentrates on accurately constructing a person's line of descent, while the family historian strives for a broader understanding of family life in the past and of the family's relations with the outside world.[4]

The word *genealogy* has been traditionally associated with individuals and groups who sought to confirm distinguished ancestors. Genealogy as a branch of history has paid little attention to the lineage of the common man. Genealogy of the African-American has been considered negligible. Three major factors account for the neglect in Afro-American genealogy. A prevailing theory has been that slavery in America disintigrated family life of blacks and distorted descendancy to the point that there could be no significant Afro-American genealogy. It is often assumed that since the majority of blacks in America before 1865 were not considered citizens, they are excluded in most public records and as such cannot be documented.

Genealogy is rooted in the national origins of a people. Designation of the genealogy of African-Americans by color as opposed to national and ancestral origins is the third factor in the neglect of Afro-American genealogy. The tendency to

---

[1]Richard Harvey, *Genealogy for Librarians* (London: Clive Bingley, 1983), p. 27.

[2]Val D. Greenwood, *The Researcher's Guide to American Genealogy* (Baltimore: Genealogical Publishing Co., 1978), p. 1.

[3]Richard Harvey, op. cit., p. 8.

[4]Allan J. Lichtman, *Your Family History* (New York: Vintage Books, 1978), p. 4.

view the black American as a phenomenon of the New World--as having come into being in 1619 without a prior history and with little to identify him except his color and the condition of slavery--ignores the true history of the people and accounts for the lack of serious consideration of African-Americans. Many books, however, have explored the rich, complex culture of precolonial Africa, and some of these books have examined customs of courtship and marriage, kinship webs, family cohesiveness, and family lineage. Complex lineage charts attest to the durability and spiritual essence of the African family. An appreciation of Afro-American genealogy and family history cannot be complete until some knowledge of African history is acquired.

Jeane E. Westin states that *genealogy* has lost its stuffy association and that *ancestor hunting* has become one of the most democratic and popular pursuits around.[5] Several factors seem to account for the rise in interest in genealogy. The civil rights movement of the 1960s raised the conscious level of ethnicity among Afro-Americans as well as other groups. The coming of the American bicentennial found many individuals and groups exploring their ancestors' roles in relation to the founding, settling, and development of America. And the success of Alex Haley's book *Roots: The Saga of an American Family* had a special impact on Afro-Americans. Haley's work has aided Afro-Americans in a better understanding of *genealogy*, its implications, and its possibilities in their lives. The majority, who had been led to believe that African descendancy research in America was virtually impossible, has come to see that not only is genealogy of the African-American possible, but also that it is probable.

Family history is not new to Afro-Americans. The family historian more than the genealogist relies on information gathered by *talking to family members*. The oral medium, a communication format historically perfected and more often preferred by the Afro-American, has preserved and perpetuated his history and lineage for centuries. The absence of written history and lineage has resulted in the loss of critical data and details: As elders have passed away and the young migrated, much genealogy has become diffused and scattered and often must be reconstructed bit by bit.

Since 1870 when the federal census of population moved to include *all* Americans in its surveys, Afro-Americans can feel assured that the name of nearly every American who was alive at the time of the survey is recorded some place.

---

[5]Jeane E. Westin, *Finding Your Roots* (Los Angeles: J.R. Tarcher, 1977), p. 7.

For decades following 1865, Afro-Americans in the south were denied access to public agencies--state and local libraries, archives, and courthouses that maintained copies of public records. Most had little perception of the genealogical value of private resources such as photographs, diaries, journals, school reports, plantation records, and church and club records found in homes and in private and public manuscript collections. Generations have lived and died unaware of the many resources available to document lineage, extend and enhance family ties, and enrich personal relationships.

With the decline of barriers to information in public agencies, another problem has been evidenced. Many of the personnel serving agencies of public information are not prepared to deal with the variables in Afro-American genealogy. Many public information assistants have had difficulty determining "how to go about" Afro-American genealogy. In a survey of one hundred librarians (graduates of accredited library schools serving as reference librarians in public agencies or college and university libraries), 87 percent indicated that they had not been introduced to Afro-American history and genealogy sources. Twelve percent indicated that they had some orientation to genealogy as a whole. Only 1 percent indicated that they had *some* orientation to Afro-American genealogy and history.

Afro-Americans continue to pursue their genealogy and they expect to find resources to aid them in their research. Having been a neglected area of concentration in local history for such a long time, resources in this area continue to be limited. The *Afro-American Genealogy Sourcebook* is intended as an aid to the Afro-American genealogy researcher and the assistant to the researcher in the following ways: in identifying background readings to better understand the African-American and the variables that impact on his genealogy, in defining types of genealogical sources, and in locating materials and agencies that have specific and potential value in Afro-American genealogy research.

PART I

BACKGROUND READING AND BASIC REFERENCE SOURCES

A. BACKGROUND READING
   1. Africa and Africans
   2. Slave Trade and Traders
   3. Black Experiences in America to 1865
   4. The Underground Railroad
   5. Slave Protests and Revolts
   6. Afro-Americans in Specific Locations
   7. The Afro-American Family
   8. Afro-American Names and Naming Practices

The history and genealogy of Afro-Americans have been misunderstood, misrepresented, and neglected due in large part to the limited early written history of Africans and the social and economic status imposed on African-Americans. Schools and textbooks, therefore, have not seriously considered the African and his descendants. As a result, the average American knows little about the history and development of Africa and the cultures of its people. Some background reading--from the ancient history of Africa to contemporary records of Afro-Americans--can help.

This section identifies selected titles to aid in an understanding of the variables that have an impact on Afro-American genealogy and in recognizing the need for and use of less traditional sources and resources in genealogy research.

1. Africa and Africans.

Bohannon, Paul, and Philip Curtin. *Africa and Africans*. Garden City, N.Y.: Natural History Press, 1971.

Discusses marriage and expansion of lineage in the African Community and the meaning of genealogy.

Curtin, Philip D. *Africa Remembered: Narratives by West Africans From the Era of the Slave Trade*.

African Genealogy

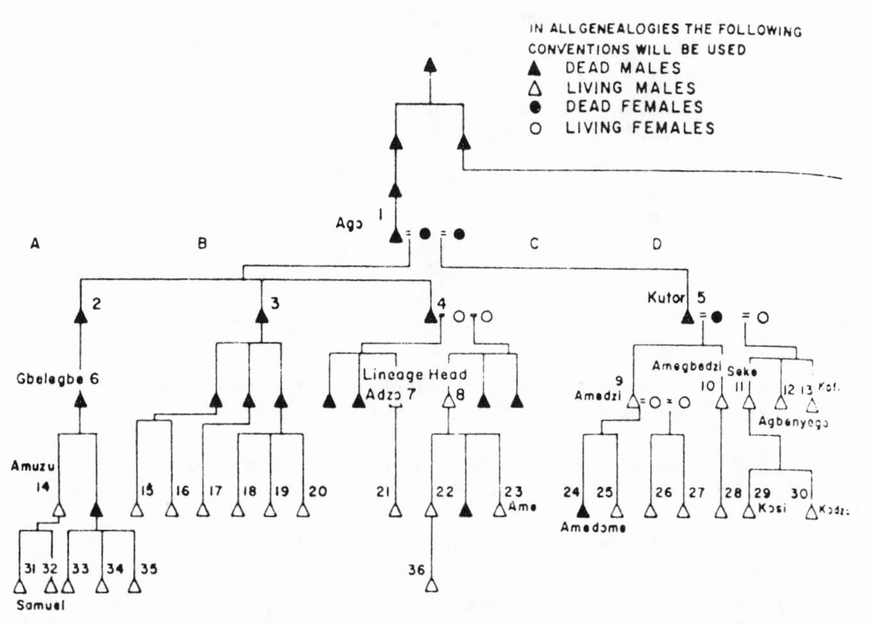

Family clusters within a section of the Amelor lineage of Woe excluding women and children

Madison, Wis.: University of Wisconsin Press, 1967.

Includes the original accounts of eight Africans who were enslaved and shipped to the coast for sales to Europeans.

Dabler, Lavinia, and William C. Brown. *Great Rulers of the African Past*. New York: Doubleday, 1965.

Story of five great African rulers and their empires.

Davidson, Basil. *The African Past*. New York: Grosset and Dunlap, 1967.

Accounts of Africa from antiquity to the present.

Degraft, Johnson, and John Coleman. *African Glory: The Story of Vanished Negro Civilizations*. New York: Praeger, 1954.

Cited as the most detailed history available of Africa and its vanished civilizations.

DuBois, W.E.B. *The World and Africa*. New York: Viking Press, 1947.

An inquiry into the part Africa has played in world history.

Flint, John E. *Nigeria and Ghana*. Englewood Cliffs, N.J.: Prentice-Hall, 1966.

Notes specific tribes indigenous to the two nations and discusses modern political affairs.

Harris, Joseph. *Africans and Their History*. New York: New American Library, 1972.

Herskovits, Melville J. *Dahomey: An Ancient West African Kingdom*. 2 vols. New York: J.J. Augustus, 1938.

A sympathetic interpretation of an ancient West African culture.

McCall, Daniel F., ed. with Norman Bennett and Jeffrey Butler. *Western African History* (Boston University Papers on Africa, vol. 4). New York: Praeger, 1968.

Contains essays on religion, politics, colonial settlers, and trade.

Murdock, George P. *Africa, Its People and Their Culture.* New York: McGraw-Hill, 1959.

Covers African ethnology.

Ottenburg, Simon. *Culture and Societies of Africa.* New York: Random House, 1970.

Destroys the myth that all African cultures are the same.

Radcliffe-Brown, Alfred R., and Daryll Forde, eds. *African Systems of Kinship and Marriage.* New York: Oxford University Press, 1950.

Discusses the broad kinship systems that link persons by interest as well as sentiment.

Samkange, Stanlake. *African Saga: A Brief Introduction to African History.* Nashville, Tenn.: Abingdon Press, 1971.

Begins with the origins of man; cites the history of the continent through the story of various nations or empires --Egypt, Ethiopia, Ghana and Mali--up to and including the slave trade of the seventeenth and eighteenth centuries and colonialism.

Turnbull, Colin. *Man in Africa: From Cairo to Cape Good Hope.* New York: Anchor Books, 1976.

Discusses African family structure, noting that a family generally consists of many members and is considered a spiritual entity.

Wierner, Leo. *Africa and the Discovery of America.* 2 vols. Philadelphia: Innes and Sons, 1920.

Deals with archaeological and etymological factors and discusses how much of the language and customs of American Indians have African sources.

Woodson, Carter G. *African Heroes and Heroines.* Washington, D.C.: Associated Publishers, 1939.

Short sketches of outstanding Africans.

Work, Monroe Nathan. *Bibliography of the Negro in Africa and America.* New York: Wilson, 1928. Reprint. New York: Argosy-Antiquarian, 1965.

Includes over 17,000 entries with an index to others.

2. Slave Trade and Traders

The Atlantic slave trade that brought Africans to America started in the year 1501. The year 1518 is documented as the beginning of the slave trade proper with the landing in the West Indies of the first black cargo direct from Africa. After 1650, with the development of the plantation system, the slave trade grew and flourished. Although Great Britain and the United States outlawed the trade in 1807, a slave cargo may have landed in the West Indies as late as the 1880s. Plantation records in the manuscript collection of Duke University's Perkins Library reveal Louisiana transactions for the purchase of slaves in the 1870s.

The forced African migration became the largest such movement in modern times. Tracking Africans and African-Americans through slave trade records reveals complex migration patterns and requires the use of a wide range of resources found in the United States and other countries, principally the countries of the West Indies. Resources include business records of former slave traders, plantation records of former slaveholders (account books), newspaper advertisements, broadsides, and legal records. Large slave traders in the South included Bolton and Dickens of Memphis, Tennessee; Eaton and Freeman of Natchez, Mississippi; Boaz, Owing, Myers, Gladden and Sexias of New Orleans, and Hector Davis and Company. Many smaller traders worked throughout the nation and particularly in the south, and their records often turn up in manuscript collections of state archives and local genealogical and historical societies. Copies of lists of slaves traded are in such collections as the New York Public Library, the Chicago Historical Society, and the Duke University Library. Miriam Wilson Foundation, the Old Slave Mart in South Carolina, and other agencies maintain an impressive collection of broadsides advertising slave trading.

Bancroft, Frederick. *Slave-Trading in the Old South.* Baltimore: J.H. Furst Co., 1930.

Cites agencies and agents and their locations in the slave trade business with copies of advertisements. New Orleans is noted as the center for such activities.

"J.W. Boaz, New Orleans, Louisiana. R. Owings, David Meyers, Gladden and Sexias, Slave Traders." *Times Picayune*, 1859-60 issues. (LaSL)

Campbell, Stanley W. *The Slave Catchers: Enforcement of the Fugitive Slave Law, 1850-1860.* Chapel Hill, N.C.:

University of North Carolina Press, 1970.

This publication includes the names of individual slaves.

"Chancery Sale of Central Bank Stock and Negroes ... Mary, Caroline, age 24; Mary, about 11; Aaron, about 17; Bernot, about 14; Rhonda, aged 30; Celia, about 15; Nat, aged 34." (Advertisement) *Weekly Montgomery* (Alabama) *Confederation*, December 10, 1859 (AlDAR).

Donnan, Elizabeth, ed. *Documents Illustrative of the History of the Slave Trade to America*. 4 vols. Washington, D.C.: Carnegie Institution of Washington, 1930-35 (Publ. no. 409). Reprint. New York: Octagon Books, 1965.

There is a list of the vessels that brought slaves to Virginia between 1710 and 1769, with the number of slaves on each and the origin of its cargo.

Dow, George Francis. *Slave Ships and Slaving*. Salem, Mass.: Marine Research Society, 1927. Reprint. Westport, Conn.: Negro University Press, 1970.

Includes excerpts from the autobiography of notorious slave trader, Captain Drake.

DuBois, W.E.B. *The Suppression of the Slave Trade*. London: Longman, Green 1896.

An account of the political struggles of the slave trade.

Eaton and Freeman, Slave Traders, Natchez, Mississippi. "Negroes for Sale." (Advertisement) *Mississippi Free Trader*, February 26, 1836 (MsDAR).

Foner, Phillip Sheldon. *Business and Slavery*. Chapel Hill, N.C.: University of North Carolina Press, 1941.

Activities of a group of northern businessmen whose fortunes were tied to southern interests.

Mannix, Daniel P., with Malcolm Cowley. *Black Cargoes: A History of the Atlantic Slave Trade, 1518-1865*. New York: Viking Press, 1962.

Chronicles the slave trade of the Atlantic coast with emphasis on the eighteenth-century slave trade. Major slaving ships of the periods, their captains, their reputations, and practices are noted.

Newton, John. *The Journal of a Slave Trader, 1750-1754, With Newton's Thoughts on the African Slave Trade.* Mystic, Conn.: Lawrence Verry, Inc., 1964.

Newton's terse, business-like entries and his reports of barter and bargaining with chiefs, traders, and middlemen betray the inhumanities of the trade.

Thomas A. Powel and Company. Auction and Commission Depot for Sale of Negroes. Montgomery, Alabama. (Advertisement) *Weekly Montgomery Confederation*, December 10, 1859. (AlSAr)

Stephenson, Wendell Holmes. *Issac Franklin: Slave Trader and Planter of the Old South.* Baton Rouge, La.: Louisiana State University Press, 1938.

Story of the plantation regime including plantation records.

Sweig, Donald M. "Reassessing the Human Dimension of the Interstate Slave Trade." *Prologue: The Journal of the National Archives*, 12: 1980.

The Thomas family sold from Alexandria, Virginia to New Orleans with three generations represented.

"To Be Sold on Thursday the Third Day of August Next, A Cargo of Ninety-Four Prime Healthy Negroes...by David and John Deas." (Broadside) July 24th, 1769. (CnHS)

White, Alonzo J., Auctioneer and Broker's List Book, 1853-63. (SCHS)

Charleston, South Carolina, firm's list of slaves belonging to various persons.

Williams, Eric. *Capitalism and Slavery.* Chapel Hill, N.C.: University of North Carolina Press, 1944.

Explains how slavery helped to finance the industrial revolution in England. Williams has much to say about white indentured servants and the enslavement of Indians.

Miriam B. Wilson Foundation. Old Slave Mart Library, Museum, Sullivans Island, S.C.

Collections of broadsides and ads of slave traders included.

3. Black Experiences in America to 1865.

Alilunas, Leo. "Fugitive Slave Cases in Ohio Prior to 1850," *Ohio State Archaeological and Historical Quarterly*, 69 (1840):160-84.

Aptheker, Herbert, ed. *A Documentary History of Negro People in the United States*. 2 vols. New York: Citadel, 1951. 1962. 1964.

Vol. I covers the period through the Civil War; Vol. II from Reconstruction to 1910.

Bell, Howard H. "Negroes in California, 1849-1859." *Phylon*, Summer 1967: 151-160.

Berlin, Ira. *Slaves without Masters*. New York: Pantheon Books, 1974.

An excellent resource for information on blacks during slavery. Includes a bibliography on resources for further study.

Blassingame, John W. *The Slave Community: Plantation Life in the Antebellum South*. New York: Oxford University Press, 1972.

Author examines the ways that blacks became enslaved, their process of acculturation in the American South, and their ties to their African heritage.

Brown, Letitia Woods, *Free Negroes in the District of Columbia, 1790-1846*. New York: Oxford University Press, 1972.

Growth of the free Negro population in the District of Columbia.

Catterall, Helen Honor Turncliff, editor. *Judicial Cases Concerning American Slavery and the Negro*. Carnegie Institute of Washington. Publication No. 374. Papers on the Division of Historical Research, 5 vols. Washington, D.C.: Carnegie Publications, 1926-37. Reprint. New York: Negro University Press, 1968.

Contains many thousands of court records on blacks and hundreds of manumission records.

Chase, Hals. "The Afro-American Migration to Haiti During the Civil War." *Phylon*, 38(1978):1.

Names of specific families who migrated may lead the researcher to specific data.

Coleman, John Winston. *Slavery Times in Kentucky*. Chapel Hill, N.C.: University of North Carolina Press, 1940. Reprint. New York: Johnson Reprint Corp., 1970.

Slavery in Kentucky including family practices and slave trading.

Dodge, D. "The Free Negro in North Carolina." *Atlantic Monthly*, 57(January 1886):20.

Dumond, Dwight Lowell. *A Bibliography of Antislavery in America*. Ann Arbor, Mich.: University of Michigan Press, 1961.

Includes works published up to the Civil War.

Franklin, John Hope. *From Slavery to Freedom: A History of American Negroes*. New York: Knopf, 1942. 2nd ed., 1956.

A comprehensive and historical landmark work.

Genovese, Eugene D. *Roll, Jordan Roll. The World the Slaves Made*. New York: Pantheon Books, 1974.

The most controversial treatment of slavery in the United States to the date of publication.

Green, Lorenzo Johnston. *The Negro in Colonial New England, 1620-1776*. New York: Columbia University Press, 1943.

Social, political, and economic repercussions of slavery upon Puritan institutions.

Harris, Norman Dwight. *The History of Negro Servitude in Illinois and of Slavery Agitation in That State, 1719-1864*. Chicago: A.C. McClurg, 1904. Reprint. New York: Haskell House, 1969. Negro University Press, 1969.

Backgrounds of the beginning of slavery in Illinois with bills of sale and registers of free blacks for many counties.

Herskovits, Melville. *The Myth of the Negro Past*. Boston: Beacon Press, 1958.

Argues that a rich, complex culture existed in precolonial Africa. Much of that culture survived depending on such factors as climate, black-white contacts, and organization and operations of plantations.

Kaplan, Sidney. *The Black Presence in the Era of the American Revolution, 1770-1800.* New York: Graphic Press, 1973.

Includes over 100 reproductions of portraits and facsimiles of diaries, letters, and other documents that record of the role of blacks throughout the revolution.

Litwack, Leon F. *North of Slavery, the Negro in the Free States, 1790-1860.* Chicago: University of Chicago Press, 1961.

The fugitive slave in the North.

Logan, Gwendolyn Evans. "The Slave in Connecticut During the American Revolution." *Connecticut Historical Society Bulletin*, 30(1965): 73-80.

McManus, Edgar J. *A History of Negro Slavery in New York.* Syracuse, N.Y.: Syracuse University Press, 1966.

Includes a biographical essay.

Mooney, Chase Curran. *Slavery in Tennessee.* Bloomington: Indiana University Press, 1957. Reprint. Westport, Conn.: Negro University Press, 1971.

Deals with the laws affecting slavery in the state;list of slave owners in 1850, and a bibliography that aids in determining plantation records still available.

Moore, George H. *Notes on the History of Slavery in Massachusetts.* New York: D. Appleton-Century, 1866. Reprint. New York: Negro University Press, 1968.

Morgan, Edmund S. *American Slavery-American Freedom: The Ordeal of Colonial Virginia.* New York: W.W. Norton, 1976.

Discusses the Americanization of the early African and the evolution of the social class that marked him.

Newman, Debra L. *List of Free Black Heads of Families in the First Census of the United States in 1790.* Washington, D.C.: 1973.

Phillips, U.B. *American Negro Slavery.* New York: Appleton, 1918.

Account of slavery in the colonies, north and south.

Postell, William D. *The Health of Slaves on Southern Plantations*. Baton Rouge, La.: Louisiana State University Press, 1951.

Includes a bibliography.

Rawick, George P. *From Sundown to Sunup: The Making of the Black Community*. *The American Slave. A Composite Autobiography*, vol. I. Westport, Conn.: Greenwood Press, 1972.

From sundown to sunup of the next working day, the American slave created behavioral and institutional bases which prevented him from becoming an absolute victim.

Scherer, Lester B. *Slavery and the Churches in Colonial America, 1619-1819*. Grand Rapids, Mich.: Wm. B. Eerdman's Co., 1975.

Suggests that the church in America was passive and permissive in regard to the dehumanization of blacks in slavery.

Seip, Terry L. "Slaves and Free Negroes in Alexandria," *Louisiana History*, Spring 1969:147-165.

Sketch of black population in Rapides Parish, Louisiana in the decade prior to the Civil War.

Sellers, James Benson. *Slavery in Alabama*. University: University of Alabama Press, 1950.

Laws, customs, and effects of slavery in Alabama.

Stampp, Kenneth M. *The Peculiar Institution: Slavery in the Antebellum South*. New York: Vintage Books, 1956.

A well-known work on the period of slavery in America including the theory of "sick paternalism."

Sydnor, Charles Sackett. *The Free Negro in Mississippi before the Civil War*. New York: Macmillan, 1927.

———. *Slavery in Mississippi*. New York: D. Appleton-Century, 1933. Reprint. Baton Rouge, La.: Louisiana State University Press, 1966. Gloucester, Mass.: Peter Smith, 1965.

Slave codes and practices reveal the dehumanizing effects of reducing people to chattel property.

Taylor, Joe G. *Negro Slavery in Louisiana.* Baton Rouge, La.: Louisiana Historical Association, 1963.

Includes a useful bibliography.

Turner, Edward Raymond. *The Negro in Philadelphia: Slavery-Servitude-Freedom, 1639-1861.* Washington, D.C.: American Historical Association, 1911. Reprint. New York: Arno Press, 1969. Negro University Press, 1969.

This essay was awarded the Justin Winsor Prize in American History for 1910.

Wade, Richard C. *Slavery in the Cities: The South, 1820-1860.* New York: Oxford University Press, 1965.

Urban slavery differed from the plantation but was equally degrading and enforced by harsh political codes, segregation, and fear.

Wright, James M. *The Free Negro in Maryland, 1634-1860.* New York: Columbia University Press, 1921. [Studies in History, Economics and Public Law]

Study of the history of free blacks in Maryland prior to the Civil War.

4. The Underground Railroad.

The Underground Railroad during the era of slavery served a vital role in aiding slaves to escape from bondage and extending migration patterns of blacks. Hundreds of individuals--free blacks, former slaves, and white abolitionists--helped the slaves escape from the south. Records of Underground Railroad activities were incriminating, and, as a consequence, few individuals kept records. William Still was one of the few exceptions. His *Underground Railroad* contained narratives, letters and copies of legal papers. While some of the fugitives from slavery stopped off in northern cities, many did not stop until they reached Canada.

The 1840s and 1850s were the height of the underground movement; and in Ontario, Canada, during these years, black communities called Dawn, Colchester, Elgin, Dresden, Windsor, Bush, Wilberforce, Riley, London and Malden were formed. As early as 1812, following the War, some blacks moved to Nova Scotia and settled a community called Africville. The Public Archives of Canada, local historical societies, and churches may have records of the communities and their inhabitants. Census records for Ontario (heads of families only) 1842; 1851(52); 1861 and 1871 (the latter three include whole families) may include blacks. Nova Scotia census records for 1861 and 1871 and later years include blacks. Since 1851, a census has been taken every ten years; however, there is no one census for the entire area. Microfilm schedules of available census records are at the Canadian Public Archives in Ottawa.

Buckmaster, Henrietta. *Let My People Go.* New York: Harper and Bros., 1941.

A comprehensive presentation of the workings of the Underground Railroad and the growth of the abolition movement.

Curtis, Anna L. *Stories of the Underground Railroad.* New York: Island Workshop Press Cooperative, 1941.

A collection of true stories.

DeArmond, Fred. "The Underground Railroad and the Missouri Borders." *Missouri Historical Review*, 37(1943):271-85.

Drew, Benjamin. *North-Side View of Slavery. The Refugee, or, The Narratives of Fugitive Slaves in Canada Related by Themselves. With an Account of the History and Condition of the Colored Population in Canada.* New York: Johnson Reprint Corp., 1948.

Narrative of blacks as told by a Boston editor.

Gara, Larry. *The Liberty Line: The Legend of the Underground Railroad*, Lexington, Ky.: University of Kentucky Press, 1961.

Asserts that free blacks, not abolitionists, carried out the rescue war.

Sibert, William. *The Underground Railroad: From Slavery to Freedom.* New York: Arno Press, 1898.

List of important fugitive slave cases.

Still, William. *The Underground Railroad: A Record of Facts, Authentic Narratives, Letters, Etc....of Slaves Themselves and Other Witnesses by the Author.* Philadelphia: Porter and Coates, 1872. Reprint. Chicago: Johnson Publishing Co., 1970. (Ebony Classic)

Includes letter from underground railroad operators and former slaves; reproductions of slave advertisements, legal papers, and newspaper articles.

Winks, Robin W. *The Blacks in Canada, A History.* Montreal, Canada: McGill-Queens University Press, 1971.

"... examines the entire range of the black experience in Canada from the 1600's to the 1970's."

5. Slave Protests and Revolts.

Aptheker, Herbert. *American Negro Slave Revolts.* New York: Columbia University Press, 1943.

Presents evidence of many conspiracies and a few rebellions from the Colonial period to the end of the Civil War.

Carroll, Joseph C. *Slave Insurrections in the United States, 1800-1865.* Boston: Chapman & Grimes, 1938. Reprint. New York: Negro University Press, 1968.

Systematic treatment of the slave insurrections that, until this book, had been given little serious attention.

Grant, Joanne, ed. *Black Protest: History, Documents, and Analysis, 1619 to the Present.* Greenwich, Conn.: Fawcett, 1968.

Documents verbal and violent reactions to slavery, discrimination, and segregation.

Katz, Jonathan. *Resistance at Christiana. The Fugitive Slave Rebellion, Christiana, Pennsylvania, September 11, 1851: A Documentary Account.* New York: Crowell, 1973.

Fugitive slaves resist a Maryland slave owner, are tried and acquitted.

Mullin, Gerald. *Flight and Rebellion. Slave Resistance in Eighteenth Century Virginia.* New York: Oxford University Press, 1972.

Attempts to assess the psychological and cultural effects of slavery.

Owens, William A. *Black Mutiny: The Revolt of the Schooner Amistad.* Philadelphia: Pilgrim Press, 1968.

The story of the heroic efforts of the slaves on the Cuban schooner to free themselves. The case came to be argued in the United States Supreme Court by John Quincy Adams.

Scott, Kenneth. "The Slave Insurrection in New York in 1712." *New York Historical Society Quarterly*, 45 January 1961: 43-74.

Tragle, Henry Irving. *The Southhampton Slave Revolt of 1831: A Compilation of Source Materials*. Amherst, Mass.: University of Massachusetts Press, 1972.

The bloodiest slave insurrection in American history, known as Nat Turner's Revolt.

Trial Records of Denmark Vesey, Introduction by John Oliver Killens. Boston: Beacon Press, 1970.

A documentation of the slave insurrection in South Carolina that planned the burning of Charleston. Contains trial transcripts, various lists, and an appendix with transcripts of the trials of four white men found guilty in the conspiracy.

6. Afro-Americans in Specific Locations.

Abajian, James de T. *Blacks and Their Contribution to the American West: A Bibliography and Union List of Library Holdings through 1970*. Boston: G.K. Hall, 1974.

Barr, Alwyn. *Black Texans: A History of the Negroes in Texas, 1528-1971*. Austin, Tex.: Jenkins Publishing, 1973.

Blassingame, John W. *Black New Orleans, 1860-1880*. Chicago: University of Chicago Press, 1973.

Writes that when rural slaves arrived in New Orleans, they had little understanding of family obligations; family disorganization existed and continued for some time.

Cooper, Zachary. *Black Settlers in Rural Wisconsin*. Madison: State Historical Society of Wisconsin, 1977.

Davis, Lenwood G. *Blacks in the Pacific Northwest, 1788-1974: A Bibliography of Published works and of Unpublished Source Materials on the Life and Contributions of Black Peoples in the Pacific Northwest*. 2nd ed. Council of Planning Libraries, Exchange Bibliography, nos. 767 and 768. Monticello, Ill.: 1975.

Useful source on black participation in the development of the region.

Davis, Russell H. *Black Americans in Cleveland, 1796-1969*. Cleveland, Ohio: The Associated Publishers, 1972.

Dubois, W.E.B. *The Philadelphia Negro. A Social Study. 1899*. New York: Schocken, 1967.

Sociological study of a black community at the end of the nineteenth century.

Franklin, Jimmie Lewis. *The Blacks in Oklahoma*. Norman, Okla.: University of Oklahoma Press, 1980.

Higgs, Julia, and Betty Lopez. *The Negro in Cambridge*. Cambridge, Mass.: Cambridge Community Relations Committee, 1946.

A study of the social and economic conditions of the black population.

Johnson, James Weldon. *Black Manhattan*. New York: Alfred A. Knopf, 1930.

"Negro life in New York City from Colonial times to date."

Kennedy, Stetson. *Palmetto County*. New York: Sloan and Pearce, 1942.

Economic, political, and social patterns found in "folksay and folktale" of lower Alabama, Georgia, and Florida.

Lapp, Rudolph. *Afro-Americans in California*. San Francisco: Boyd and Fraser Publishing, 1979.

Mabry, William A. *The Negro in North Carolina Politics Since Reconstruction*. Durham, N.C.: Duke University Press, 1940.

A paper delivered at the Trinity College Historical Society meeting.

McCloy, Shelby T. *The Negro in the French West Indies*. Lexington, Ky.: University of Kentucky Press, 1966.

Emphasizes social and cultural history that marked blacks in the French West Indies.

National Urban League. *A Study of the Social and Economic Conditions of the Negro Population, Charleston, South Carolina*. Conducted for the Welfare Council. March-April, 1946.

One typescript volume maintained by the South Carolina Historical Society.

Perdue, Robert E. *The Negro in Savannah, 1865-1900.* New York: Exposition Press, 1973.

Includes a list of free blacks in Savannah and a bibliography.

Rice, Lawrence D. *The Negro in Texas, 1874-1900.* Baton Rouge, La.: Louisiana State University Press, 1971.

Deals with bigotry and blacks' roles in politics, social progress, and agriculture.

Robertson, Clara Hamlet. *Kansas Territorial Settlers of 1860 Who Were Born in Tennessee, North Carolina, and South Carolina.* Baltimore: Genealogical Publishing Co., 1976.

Rousseve, Charles B. *The Negro in Louisiana.* New Orleans: Xavier University Press, 1937.

Aspects of the history and literature of black Louisianans.

Strona, Proserfina A. *Blacks in Hawaii: A Bibliography.* Honolulu, Hawaii: Pacific Unit, State Library Branch, 1975.

Acknowledges and documents the black presence in the "Aloha State."

Taylor, A.A. *The Negro in Tennessee, 1865-1880.* Washington, D.C.: Associated Publishers, 1941.

Political, economic, and social condition of Negroes in Tennessee during the Reconstruction period.

Thurman, Sue Bailey. *Pioneers of Negro Origin in California.* San Francisco: Acme Publishing, 1971.

United States Works Projects Administration. *The Negro in Virginia.* New York: Hastings House, 1940.

The American Negro from 1619 to the present.

———. *The Negroes of Nebraska.* Lincoln, Neb.: Woodruff Printing Co., 1940.

"... an attempt to highlight the entire picture of Negro life in the State of Nebraska."

———. State of Arkansas, Writers' Program and Urban League of Greater Little Rock, Sponsers. *Survey of Negroes in Little Rock and North Little Rock*. Little Rock, Ark.: The Urban League, 1941.

A socioeconomic study of local conditions.

Washington State Library, Olympia. *The Negro in the State of Washington, 1788-1969: A Bibliography of Published Works and Unpublished Source of Materials on the Life and Achievements of the Negro in the Evergreen State*. Olympia, Wash.: The Library, 1968.

Winks, Robin. *The Blacks in Canada, A History*. Montreal, Canada: McGill-Queens University Press, 1971.

"... examines the entire range of the black experience in Canada from the 1600's to the 1970's."

Woodson, Carter G. *The Rural Negro*. Washington, D.C.: Association for the Study of Negro Life and History, 1930.

Conditions of blacks in the rural south.

Wright, R. *The Negro in Pennsylvania: A Study in Economic History*. Philadelphia: Christian Recorder, 1912.

7. The Afro-American Family.

Bigham, Darrel. "The Black Family in Evansville and Panderburgh County, Indiana in 1880." *Indiana Magazine of History*, 75(1979).

Good source on black families in the West.

Billingsley, Andrew. *Black Families in White America*. Englewood Cliffs, N.J.: Prentice-Hall, 1966.

Descriptions of major dimensions of Negro family life--the problems and potentials associated with different patterns.

Blassingame, John W. *The Slave Community: Plantation Life in the Antebellum South*. New York: Oxford University Press, 1972.

Cansler, Charles W. *Three Generations: The Story of a Colored Family of Eastern Tennessee*. Kingsport, Tenn.: Kingsport Press, 1939.

Focuses on three generations of a family beginning in North Carolina.

Daniel, Constance E.H. "Two North Carolina Families--The Harrises and the Richardsons." *Negro History Bulletin*, 13(October 1949): 3-12.

Accounts of these families are drawn from the records of Virginia Richardson McGuire.

Davis, Arthur P. "William Roscoe Davis and His Descendants." *Negro History Bulletin*, 13(January 1950): 75-79.

Davis, Lenwood G. *Black Families in the United States: A Selected Bibliography*. Westport, Conn.: Greenwood Press, 1978.

Includes materials on the black family from slavery to the present.

Day, Carolina [Bond]. *A Study of Some Negro-White Families in the United States*. Cambridge, Mass.: Peabody Museum of Harvard University, 1932. Reprint. Westport, Conn.: Negro University Press, 1970.

Statistical materials primarily taken from families living in the southeastern section of the United States.

Dubois, W.E.B. *The Negro American Family. 1908*. New York: Negro University Press, 1969.

Includes the proceedings of the 1908 conference for the Study of Negro Problems, Atlanta University.

Estabrook, Arthur Howard. *Mongrel Virginians: The Win Tribe*. Baltimore: Williams and Wilkins Co., 1926.

Discusses a group of people of mixed blood who resided in the foothills of the Blue Ridge Mountains, Virginia.

Frazier, E. Franklin. *The Negro Family in Chicago*. Chicago: University of Chicago Press, 1932.

This controversial first major work by Franklin includes an introduction by E.W. Burgess.

———. *The Negro Family in the United States*. Chicago: University of Chicago Press, 1939.

Franklin argues that poor urban black families live in communities where institutional life has disappeared.

Gibson, William. *Family Life and Morality: Studies in Black and White*. Washington, D.C.: University Press of America, 1980.

Author posits that social, psychological, and economic forces have victimized and impeded the black community.

Goldstein, Rhoda L. ed. *Black Life and Culture in the United States*. New York: Thomas Y. Crowell, 1971.

Articles by various authors developed from lectures delivered in a course at Douglass College, Spring 1970.

Gutman, Herbert. *The Black Family in Slavery and Freedom, 1750-1925*. New York: Pantheon, 1976.

A significant work that disputes earlier theories of black family disintegration. Reconstruction of family lineage from slave records.

Haley, Alex. *Roots: The Saga of an American Family*. New York: Doubleday, 1976.

Alex Haley traces his family roots back to its African origins.

Hill, Robert B. *Strength of Black Families*. New York: Emerson Hall, 1971. 1972.

Lewis, Hylan. "The Changing Negro Family," in Eli Ginzberg, ed. *The Nation's Children*. Vol. I. New York: Columbia University Press, 1960.

Points out that the new task of the Negro family is to prepare its members to live in a desegregated world.

McAdoo, Harriette Pipes. *Black Families*. Beverly Hills, Calif.: Sage Publications, 1981.

Looks at all aspects of black families including economic factors and mobility.

Merritt, Carole. "Slave Family History Records: An Abundance of Materials." *Georgia Archives*, 6(Spring 1978): 16-21.

Public as well as private documents are explored.

Morgan, Kathryn L. *Children of Strangers: The Stories of a Black Family*. Philadelphia: Temple University Press, 1980.

Deals with the author's transcriptions of statements about her family in Lynchburg, Virginia.

Murray, Pauli. *Proud Shoes: The Story of an American Family*. New York: Harper & Row, 1978.

Four generations of American black families are merged in this work. Earlier edition, 1956.

"A Remarkable Negro Family." *Southern Workman*, October 1925.

Spotlights the story of the Hubert family of Springfield, Georgia.

Roberts, J. Deotis. *Roots of a Black Future: Family and Church*. White Plains, N.Y.: Westminster Press, 1976.

This work brings the black family and church together from a theological point of view.

Rogers, Louise F. *The Older Black Families of Rogersville, Tennessee*. Rogersville, Tenn.: Louise Rogers, 1974.

A native daughter documents black family history in her hometown.

Rose, James M., and Barbara Brown. *Tapestry: A Living History of the Black Family in Southeastern Connecticut*. New London, Conn.: New London Historical Society, 1979.

Stack, Carol B. *All Our Kin: Strategies for Survival in a Black Community*. New York: Harper and Row, 1974.

Discusses social conditions of blacks and black families throughout history. However, names are changed to avoid recognition.

Staples, Robert. "The Myth of Black Matriarchy." *The Black Scholar*, 2(June 1971): 2-9.

Looks at the myth of the impotent black male.

Sutton's History of Creed Freedmen Families, compiled by the Oklahoma Historical Society, Oklahoma City.

A work that was developed from the final allotment (Dawes) census card information.

Thompson, Ezra Bell. "Vaughn Family: A Tale of Two Continents." *Ebony*, 30(February 1975): 53-58.

Family history of descendants of former American slave, Scipio Vaughn.

United States Department of Labor. Office of Policy Planning and Research. *The Negro Family: The Case for National Action*. Washington, D.C.: GPO, 1965. Reprint. Westport, Conn.: Greenwood Press, 1981.

Reprint of the controversial study on the black family.

Williams, Roger M. *The Bonds: An American Family*. New York: Atheneum, 1971.

Story of the Bond family that includes Horace Mann Bond, educator and Julian Bond, State Senator.

Williams, Robert C. *Marriage and Family Relations*. New York: John Wiley and Sons, 1972.

Chapter Four deals with ethnic groups including the development of the black family.

Willie, Charles V. *The Family Life of Black People*. Columbus, Ohio: Charles E. Merrill, 1970.

8. Afro-American Names and Naming Practices.

Barker, Howard F. "The Family Names of American Negroes." *American Speech*, 14(October 1939): 163-74.

Beers, H. Dwight. "African Names and Naming Practices: A Selected List of References in English." *Library of Congress Information Bulletin*. 36(25 March 1977): 206-7.

Limited in scope, this reference is a sample of the subject collected in the Library of Congress' African Section.

Chuk-Orijii, Ogonna. *Names from Africa*. Chicago: Johnson Publishing Co., 1972.

Dillard, Joey Lee. *Black Names: Contributions to the Sociology of Language*. The Hague: Mouton, 1976.

The etymology of names frequently associated with blacks is discussed in this work.

Gutman, Herbert. *The Black Family in Slavery and Freedom, 1750-1925*. New York: Pantheon, 1976.

The chapter, "Somebody Knows My Name," discusses naming practices of Afro-Americans.

McKinzie, Harry, and Issy K. Tindimwebwa. *Names from East Africa: Their Meaning and Pronunciation*. Los Angeles: McKinzie Publ., 1980.

Compilation of both male and female names from East Africa: Kenya, Uganda, Tanzania, and Rwanda. Pronunciations, meanings, and the tribe and country of origin are included.

Madubiuke, Ihechukwa. *A Handbook of African Names*. Washington, D.C.: Three Continents Press, 1976.

Puckett, Newbell Niles. *Black Names in America: Origins and Usage*, edited by Murray Heller. Boston: G.K. Hall, 1975.

Lists and discusses names common among free blacks and blacks in slavery beginning in the seventeenth century and extending through the mid-1940s.

Sonyikan, Becktimbia. *Know and Claim Your African Name*. Dayton, Ohio: Rucker Publishing, 1975.

Encourages the reclaiming of African names by Afro-Americans.

Thomas, Kenneth H., Jr. "A Note on the Pitfalls of Black Genealogy: The Origins of Black Surnames." *Georgia Archives*, 6(Spring 1978): 623-30.

Discusses the inconsistencies in the appearance of names in records.

B. BASIC REFERENCE SOURCES, AFRO-AMERICANA
  1. Biographical Sources
  2. Bibliographies, Guides, and Directories by and about Afro-Americans
  3. Newspapers

General reference questions including inquiries about Afro-Americans are often initial steps into genealogy research. Sources utilized include factbooks, bibliographies, biographies, directories, histories, and studies. Newspapers are a major source of current and retrospective information about people, places, and events in the Afro-American experience, and they are included in this section

1. Biographical Sources.

Bacote, Samuel Williams, ed. *Who's Who among Colored Baptists of the United States*. Kansas City: Franklin Hudson, 1913.

Brignano, Russell Carl. *Black Americans in Autobiography: An Annotated Bibliography of Autobiographies and Autobiographical Books Written since the Civil War*. Durham, N.C.: Duke University Press, 1974.

Dictionary of American Negro Biography, edited by Rayford W. Logan and Michael R. Winston. New York: W.W. Norton, 1982.

"Comprehensive biographical dictionary based on scholarly research."

Peters, Margaret. *The Ebony Book of Black Achievement*. Chicago: Johnson Publishing, 1974.

Includes twenty-six outstanding biographical sketches that illustrate black achievement from the fourteenth to the twentieth century.

Scally, Sister Mary Anthony. *Negro Catholic Writers, 1900-1943*. Detroit: Walter Romig, 1945.

Biographies as well as lists of works of each author.

Southern, Eileen. *Biographical Dictionary of Afro-American Musicians*. Westport, Conn.: Greenwood Press, 1982.

Spradling, Mary, ed. *In Black and White: Afro-Americans in Print.* Kalamazoo, Mich.: Public Library, 1976.

Includes in the index the names of more than 150 slave-born Afro-Americans along with 7,000 other names.

Toppin, Edgar Allan. *A Biographical History of Blacks in America since 1528.* New York: McKay, 1971

Narrative history based largely upon biographical sources.

Who's Who Among Negro Lawyers, compiled and edited by Sadie T.M. Alexander. Philadelphia: National Bar Association, 1945.

Names, addresses, and brief biographies of Negro lawyers who were members of the Association in 1945.

Who's Who in Colored America: A Biographical Dictionary of Notable Living persons of Negro Descent in America, 1928-29. Edited by Joseph J. Bores. New York: Who's Who in Colored America Corp., 1927. 1929.

Williams, Ethel L. *Biographical Directory of Negro Ministers.* Metuchen, N.J.: Scarecrow Press, 1965.

This work includes biographical data and a bibliography on suggested sources for further information.

2. Bibliographies, Guides, Directories by and About Afro-Americans.

Abajian, James de T. *Blacks in Selected Newspapers, Censuses, and Other Sources: An Index to Names and Subjects.* Boston: G.K. Hall, 1977, 3 vols.

Afro-Americana, 1553-1906. Author Catalog of the Library, County of Philadelphia and the Historical Society of Pennsylvania. Boston: G.K. Hall, 1973.

A useful guide to a wide range of sources helpful in black genealogy research.

American Missionary Association. Archives, 1839-82. (AmRC)

This collection of important records of the abolitionist organization relates to missionary work in the south after the Civil War to the beginnings of black higher education in the south. Microfilm copies of approximately 350,000 manuscript pieces from this collection may be found in the Center for Research Libraries, Chicago.

Aptheker, Herbert, ed. *A Documentary History of the Negro People in the United States from Colonial Times to the Founding of the NAACP in 1910*. New York: Citadel Press, 1951.

Bentley, George R. *A History of the Freedmen's Bureau*. Philadelphia: Octagon Books, 1970.

Guide and evaluation of the Bureau's records, leading to vital statistics of blacks included in the records.

Black American Reference Book, edited by Mabel Smythe. Sponsored by the Phelps-Stokes Fund. Englewood Cliffs, N.J.: Prentice-Hall, 1976.

Based on the *American Negro Reference Book, 1965*. Brings together information on black Americans' history, social, and economic status as well as scholarly articles.

Brawley, Benjamin. *A Social History of the American Negro, Being a History of the Negro Problem in the United States Including a History and Study of the Republic of Liberia*. New York: Macmillan, 1921.

A major work in Afro-American history.

Catalogue of Records of Black Organizations in Alabama. Compiled by the Collection and Evaluation of Materials about Black Americans Program of the Alabama Center for Higher Education. Birmingham, Ala.: Center for Higher Education, 1979.

Listing of 239 black organizations in Alabama including churches, civic, social, professional, burial associations; minutes of meetings and rosters of members, and oral history sources.

Catterall, Helen Honor Turncliff, ed. *Judicial Cases Concerning American Slavery and the Negro*. Carnegie Institution of Washington Publication No. 374. 1926-37. Reprint. New York: Negro University Press, 1968.

Includes thousands of court records and manumission records of blacks.

Clarke, Robert L. *Afro-American History: Sources for Research*. Washington, D.C.: Howard University Press, 1981.

Useful in identifying resources for extended research.

Connecticut Historical Society. *Bibliography of Materials to Be Found in the Connecticut Historical Society on Black People in Connecticut and New England.* The Society, [n.d.]

Bibliography may be available on request.

J.K. Daniels Library, Lane College, Jackson, Tenn. *Negro Collection: A Bibliography.* 1965.

Library's collection holds significant papers on Bishop Issac Lane, founder of the Christian Methodist Episcopal Church.

Directory of Historical Societies and Agencies in the United States and Canada. Nashville, Tenn.: American Association for State and Local History. Biennial.

A complete guide to historical societies, which are a valuable source of often otherwise unidentified local materials contained in private collections.

Disciples of Christ Historical Society. *Preliminary Guide to Black Materials in the Disciples of Christ Historical Society.* Nashville, Tenn.: 1971.

Bibliography on holdings of black materials in the Society's collection. Also available on microfilm.

Donald, Henderson H. *Negro Freedman: Life Conditions of the American Negro in the Early Years after Emancipation.* New York: Schumann, 1952.

Study of freed slaves during the early years of reconstruction.

Drotning, Phillip T. *A Guide to Negro History in America.* Garden City, N.Y.: Doubleday, 1968.

"A geographic guide of the Negro's contribution to America."

Dubois, W.E.B. *The Souls of Black Folk.* Greenwich, Conn.: Fawcett, 1966.

Expresses desire for a militant movement among blacks.

Encyclopedia of Black America. Edited by W. Augusta Law and Virgil A. Clift. New York: McGraw-Hill, 1980.

Famous Facts about Negroes, edited by Romeo B. Gantt. New York: Arno Press, 1972.

List of little known facts about Afro-Americans including contributions to society.

Fishel, Leslie, and Benjamin Quarles. *The Negro American: A Documentary History*. Atlanta: Scott, Foresman, 1967.

Traces the history of Afro-Americans from Africa to the 1960s.

Franklin, John Hope, and Isidore Starr, editors. *The Negro in Twentieth Century America*. New York: Vintage Books, 1967.

A reader on the struggle for civil rights.

Frazier, E. Franklin. *Black Bourgeoise*. New York: The Free Press, 1965.

A tract in which the author castigates the black middle class.

Genealogical and Local History Books in Print. Springfield, Va.: Genealogical Books in Print, 1981.

Section on Afro-Americans is limited, but the work includes a wide range of general sources.

Gleason, Eliza. *The Southern Negro and the Public Library*. Chicago: University of Chicago Press, 1941.

"The first full-length study of public library services to the southern Negro."

Hale, Richard W., Jr. *Guide to Photocopied Historical Materials in the United States and Canada*. Ithaca, N.Y.: Cornell University Press, 1961.

A guide to the location of such records as census reports, government, state, town and business reports.

Hampton Normal and Agricultural Institute, Virginia. Collis R. Huntington Library. *A Classified Catalogue of the Negro Collection*, compiled by the Writers Program of Works Project Administration in the State of Virginia. Hampton, Va.: 1941.

Catalogue of the library's holdings on Negro materials.

Index to Periodical Articles by and about Negroes (the successor to the *Guide to Negro Periodical Literature*). Compiled by A.P. Marshall. Xenia, Ohio: Central State University, 1950- .

Prepared jointly by the staffs of Central State and the Schomburg Collection, this publication is issued at irregular intervals.

Johnson, Clifton. "Some Archival Sources on Negro History in Tennessee." *Tennessee Historical Quarterly*, 18(Winter 1969): 297-416.

National Cyclopedia of the Colored Race. Montgomery, Ala.: National Publishing Co., 1919.

Covers subjects of education, churches, and national fraternal organizations.

Negro Almanac: A Reference Work on the Afro-American. 4th ed. Compiled by Harry A. Ploski and James Williams. New York: John Wiley, 1983.

Information on a wide range of topics on Afro-Americans including a chronology of events in the lives of Afro-Americans.

New York Public Library Research Libraries. *Dictionary Catalog of the Local History and Genealogical Division.* 18 vols. Boston: G.K. Hall, 1974.

Peterson, Clarence Stewart. *Consolidated Bibliography of the County Histories in Fifty States in 1961*. Baltimore: Genealogical Publishing Co., 1973.

A guide to county histories of the United States with descriptions of lifestyles during specific periods.

Porter, Dorothy B. "Documentation on the Afro-American: Familiar and Less Familiar Sources." *African Studies Bulletin*, December 1969.

Porter, Dorothy B. *The Negro in the United States: A Selected Bibliography*. Washington, D.C.: Library of Congress, 1970.

Selected bibliography covering a wide range of topics.

Schatz, Walter, ed. *Directory of Afro-American Resources.* New York: Bowker, 1970.

A useful guide to collections of interest to Afro-Americans. Genealogical resources included in public and private collections.

Woodson, Carter G. *A Century of Negro Migration.* Washington, D.C.: Associated Publishers, 1918.

Migration of Afro-Americans during and after the Civil War and the great migration of the World War period.

———. *Education of the Negro Prior to 1861.* New York: G.P. Putnam's Sons, 1951.

"History of the Afro-American in the United States from the beginning of slavery to the Civil War."

Work, Monroe Nathan. *Bibliography of the Negro in Africa and America.* New York: Wilson, 1928. Reprint. New York: Argosy-Antiquarian, 1965.

Includes over 17,000 entries with an index to other sources.

3. Newspapers.

American Newspapers, 1821-1936. A Union List of Files Available in the United States and Canada. Edited by Winfred Gregory under the auspices of the Bibliographical Society of America. New York: H.W. Wilson Co., 1937.

A Union List of newspapers in nearly 5,700 depositories such as courthouses and private collections.

Brown, Warren Henry. *Checklist of Negro Newspapers in the United States, 1827-1946.* Jefferson City, Mo.: Lincoln University, 1946.

An essential guide to the location of black newspapers.

Daniel, Walter C. *Black Journals of the United States.* Westport, Conn.: Greenwood Press, 1982. (Historical Guides to the World's Periodicals and Newspapers)

Approximately 100 publications are reviewed with a descriptive overview and historical background on each work.

Directory of U.S. Negro Newspapers, Magazines and Periodicals. New York: U.S. Negro World, 1966.

Index to Indianapolis Daily Newspapers. 1898-(to date.) (IndSL)

An index by subject, organization, and name. Prominent blacks are listed in alphabetical order.

LaBrie, Henry G. *The Black Newspaper in America: A Guide.* 3rd ed. Kennebunkport, Maine: Mercer House Press, 1973.

———. *A Survey of Black Newspapers in America.* Kennebunkport, Maine: Mercer House Press, 1979.

Updated version of the 1970 survey of newspapers under title, *The Black Press in America: A Guide.*

Moorland-Spingarn Research Center. Howard University, Washington, D.C.: *Black Press Archives and Gallery of Distinguished Newspaper Publishers* (pamphlet), [n.d.].

The Center receives more than two hundred current black American, African, and Caribbean newspapers and holds more than 400 titles on microfilm.

Myers, Rex C. "Montana's Negro Newspapers, 1894-1911." *Montana Journalism Review,* 16:1973.

Lists black newspapers published in the state.

Oklahoma Historical Society. Division of Library Resources. Newspaper Department. *Black Newspapers.* Oklahoma City: The Society (OkHS).

A list of newspapers with black publications underlined to include the *Black Dispatch,* the oldest continuous black newspaper in America.

Pride, Armistead Scott. *Negro Newspapers on Microfilm: A Selected List.* Washington, D.C.: Library of Congress, Photoduplication Service, 1953.

Simpson, George E. *The Negro in the Philadelphia Press.* Philadelphia: University of Philadelphia Press, 1936.

Evaluation and analysis of news about the Negro in the Philadelphia press.

C. BASIC GENEALOGY REFERENCE SOURCES
1. Bibliographies, Periodical Guides, and Directories
2. "How-to-Do" Genealogy Research
3. Oral History

A wide variety of resources are utilized in genealogy research. Certain resources, however, have been designed especially for the purposes of *genealogy*. The references in this section include some major guides and directories, books and articles that are concerned with or are recognized as major genealogical references. Also included are resources on methods, procedures, and techniques in Afro-American genealogy. Oral history is treated separately since this medium assumes a role in Afro-American genealogy that is unparalleled in other genealogical pursuits.

1. Bibliographies, Periodical Guides, and Directories.

Biography and Genealogy Master Index. 2nd ed. 1981-82. Supplement, 1982, edited by Miranda C. Herbert and Barbara McNeil. Detroit: Gale Research, 1980. (Gale Biographical Index Series, no. 1).

"A consolidated index to more than 3,200 biographical sketches."

Black Genealogy: Sources of Black Genealogical Records. Videorecording (WGTV). Atlanta, Ga.: Georgia: Center for Continuing Education, 1977.

Includes records from churches, courthouses, relief societies, the Freedmen's Bureau, and others.

Burnett, Helen Louise. "Black Genealogy: The Quest for History." *Journal of Genealogy*, January 1977: 12-13.

Carroll, (Mrs.) Riernan J. "Sources for Genealogical Research in State Department Records." *National Genealogical Society Quarterly*, 52(December 1964).

Ethnic Genealogy: A Research Guide, edited by Jessie Carney Smith. Westport, Conn.: Greenwood Press, 1983.

A series of papers based on the Institute in Ethnic Genealogy held at Fisk University, Summer 1979.

Greenwood, Val D. *The Researcher's Guide to American Genealogy*. Baltimore: Genealogical Publ. Co., 1973.

General methods in genealogy with definitions and references that make it a valuable reference tool.

Hale, Richard W., Jr. *Guide to Photocopied Historical Materials in the United States and Canada*. Ithaca, N.Y.: Cornell University Press, 1961

A guide to the location of census records: city, state, church, business, and other records.

Harvey, Richard. *Genealogy for Librarians*. London: Clive Bingley, 1983.

Although this work concentrates on English sources, Chapter 1 has an interesting discussion on the librarian and the genealogist.

Index to American Genealogies and to Genealogical Materials Contained in All Works as Town Histories, County Histories, Local Histories, Historical Society Publications, Biographies, Historical Periodicals, and Kindred Works. Albany, N.Y.: Munsell, 1900-08. Reprint. Baltimore: Genealogical Publishing Co., 1967.

While not specifically designed for the Afro-American genealogist, this work like some other basic references, can be useful in black genealogy research.

Johnson, Clifton H. "Some Archival Sources in Negro History in Tennessee." *Tennessee Historical Quarterly*, Winter 1969: 297-316.

Kaminkow, Marion J., ed. *Genealogies in the Library of Congress: A Bibliography*. 3 vols. Baltimore: Magna Carta Book Co., 1972.

"A guide to the genealogical monographs which may be found in the Library of Congress and other libraries."

———, editor. *United States Local Histories in the Library of Congress*. 5 vols. Baltimore: Magna Carta Book Co., 1975.

Includes all of the books cataloged and classified under the local history portion of the Library of Congress classification scheme.

Kirkman, E. Kay. *Counties of the United States and Their Genealogical Value*. Salt Lake City, Utah: Deseret Book Co., 1964.

Notes counties that have been divided with original and current names.

———. *A Handy Guide to Record Searching in the Larger Cities of the United States*. Logan, Utah: Everton Publs., 1974.

Newberry Library. Chicago, Illinois. *The Genealogical Index*. Boston: G.K. Hall, 1960.

A complete index of all published family genealogies owned by the Newberry Library as of 1918.

Parker, J. Carlyle. *Library Service for Genealogists*. Detroit: Gale Research Co., 1981. (vol. 15, Gale Genealogy and Local History Series)

Many of the titles included in this bibliography help to identify additional sources.

Schreiner-Yantis, Netti, ed. *Genealogical Books in Print*. 2 vols. Springfield, Va.: 1975.

Includes section on books on Afro-American genealogy.

The Source: A Guidebook of American Genealogy, edited by Arlene Eakle and Johni Cerny. Salt Lake City, Utah: Ancestry Publishing Co., 1984.

"A guide to a vast range of genealogical sources."

A chapter is devoted to research on each of several ethnic groups including Afro-Americans.

Spear, Dorothy N. *Bibliography of American Directories through 1860*. Worchester, Mass.: American Antiquarian Society, 1961.

A list of city and business directories through 1860 with most of the directories on microfilm at the Brooklyn Public Library.

Stemmons, J.D. *United States Compendium*. Logan, Utah: Everton Publs., 1973.

An excellent source of information on census records.

United States National Archives and Records Service. *Directory of Archives and Manuscripts Repositories*. Washington, D.C.: 1978.

United States Guide to Genealogical Research in the National Archives. Washington, D.C.: National Archives Trust Fund Board, 1983.

Intended as a revision of the 1964 volume, it is rewritten and expanded with special records relating to specific groups including Afro-Americans.

United States Works Projects Administration. *Inventory of Parish Archives of Louisiana*. New Orleans: Historical Records Survey, 1940.

Useful in locating and identifying early parish records in the state.

Periodical Guides.

Genealogical periodicals contain a wealth of information, including descendancy data, family histories, family sketches, indexes to otherwise unindexed records, information on private collections, genealogical inquiries, locality histories, and copies of records. Periodical indexes useful in identifying genealogical periodicals include:

Genealogical Periodical Annual Index, edited by Ellen Stanley Rogers and George Ely Russell. Bladenburg and Bowie, Md.: Genealogical Recorders. (Annual, 1962-present)

Jacobus, Donald Lines. *Index to Genealogical Periodicals*. 3 vols. Baltimore: Genealogical Publishing Co., 1932-1953.

Index is by family name, place, and topic.

Standard Periodical Directory. Lexington, N.Y.: Oxbridge Comm. (Annual, 1964-1965)

Easy-to-use, more complete lists of genealogical periodicals and includes same information as specialized lists.

Ulrich's International Periodicals Directory. New York: R.R. Bowker, (1947-present)

Includes a list of genealogical periodicals with up-to-date information and, like the *Standard Periodical Directory*, includes same information as specialized lists.

2. "How-to-Do" Genealogy Research

Beard, Timothy Field, and Denise Demong. *How to Find Your Family Roots*. New York: McGraw-Hill, 1977.

Includes one chapter on methods of searching black ancestry and a list of resources that aid in the search.

Blockson, Charles, and Ron Fry. *Black Genealogy*. Englewood Cliffs, New Jersey: Prentice-Hall, 1977.

Subtitled, "How to discover your own family's roots and trace your ancestors back through an eventful past...."

Burgen, Michele. "How to Trace Your Family Tree." *Ebony*, 32(July 1977): 52-54.

Practical methods for the Afro-American family researcher.

Doane, Gilbert H. *Searching for Your Ancestors: The How and Why of Genealogy*. 4th ed. Minneapolis: University of Minnesota Press, 1973.

A well-written, fundamental guide in basic genealogical techniques.

Draznin, Yaffa. *The Family Historian's Handbook*. New York: Jove/HBJ Book, 1978.

"Special Searching Problems of Blacks" on pages 114-122, and the section, "The Library: General and Genealogical," are especially relevant.

Everton, George B., and Gunnar Rasmuson. The Handy Book for Genealogists. 6th ed. rev. and enl. Logan, Utah: Everton Publishers, 1970.

Useful for addresses of courthouses and their records of interest to genealogists.

Hathaway, Beverly W. *Genealogy Research Sources in Tennessee*. West Jordan, Utah: Estates Research Co., 1972.

Useful source for the Tennessee researcher.

How to Trace Your Family Tree. By the American Genealogical Research Staff. Garden City, N.Y.: Doubleday, 1975.

"What is available from local, state, and federal government sources."

Reed, Robert D. *Where and How to Research Your Ethnic American Cultural Heritage: Black Americans*. Saratoga, Calif.: The Author, 1979.

Roderick, Thomas H. "Negro Genealogy." *The American Genealogist*, 47: 1971.

Notes the variables in Afro-American genealogy.

Rose, James, and Alice Eichholz. *Black Genesis*. Detroit: Gale, 1978.

A valuable work including materials identified in a survey of primary and secondary Afro-American genealogy sources in the United States.

Scarupa, Harriet Jackson. "Black Genealogy." *Essence*, 7(July 1976): 56-57, 84-87.

Walker, James D. *Black Genealogy: How to Begin*. Athens, Ga.: University of Georgia Center for Continuing Education, 1977.

A small but useful guide in beginning genealogy.

———. Black History Resources in United States Military Records. World Conference on Records: Preserving Our Heritage, August 12-15, 1980. V. 4, Part 2, no. 239. Salt Lake City, Utah: Church of the Latter-Day Saints.

Exploration of resources found among military records that are useful to the Afro-American genealogist.

Westin, Jeanne Eddy. *Finding Your Roots: How Every American Can Trace His Ancestors at Home and Abroad*. Los Angeles: J.P. Tarcher, 1977.

Guide in basic genealogical techniques with sections of special interest to ethnic minorities including Afro-Americans.

Whiteman, Maxwell. "Black Genealogy: Problems, Sources, Methodology." *Reference Quarterly: 11* (Summer 1972): 311-19.

Young, Tommie Morton. *African-American Genealogy: Exploring and Documenting the Black Family*. Clarksville, Tenn.: Josten Publishers, 1982.

Includes suggested activities for the beginning genealogy researcher.

———. "Ten Steps in Rooting Out the Past of the Black Family." *North Carolina Genealogical Society Journal*, 6 (no. 3, August 1980): 150-61.

Part I of an article outlining steps in Afro-American genealogy research.

3. Oral History

All These Things Are Us. (videotape) Edited by Margaret Pollard and Gertrude Turrentine with Donna Benson. Moncure, N.C.: Funded by the North Carolina Humanities Committee, 1979.

Oral interviews with the descendants of the founders of the post-Civil War, all-black town of Moncure, N.C.

Allen, Barbara, and Lynwood Montell. *From Memory to History: Using Oral Sources in Local Historical Research.* Nashville: American Association for State and Local History, 1981.

Deals with oral history and includes application to genealogical research.

The American Slave: A Composite Autobiography. Edited by George Rawick. Westport, Conn.: Greenwood Press, 1972. 19 vols. (Contributions in Afro-American and African Studies, No. 11)

Invaluable narrative source for the study of slavery. Interviews with ex-slaves present a picture of slavery and slave culture that earlier studies do not provide. Family relations are revealed.

The American Slave: A Composite Autobiography. Supplement Series I. George P. Rawick, General Editor. Westport, Conn.: Greenwood Press, (1977) 12 vols. (Contributions in Afro-American and African Studies, No. 35)

Supplementary series of narratives to the interviews of ex-slaves conducted under the auspices of the Federal Writer's Project in the 1930s.

Baum, Willa K. *Oral History for the Local Historical Society.* Stockton, Calif.: Conference of California Historical Societies, 1969.

Uses of oral history in local history research.

Cooper, G.C. "Oral Tradition in African Societies." *Negro History Bulletin*, 46(October-December 1983): 101-03.

Cutting-Baker, Amy Kotkin, and Margaret Yocum. *Family Folklore: Interviewing Guide and Questionnaire.* Washington, D.C.: GPO. New York: Simon and Schuster, 1978.

Techniques in interviewing for family history research.

Epstein, Ellen R., and Rona Mendelsohn. *Record and Remember: Tracing Your Roots through Oral History.* New York: Sovereign Books, 1978.

How the oral medium can reveal basic information in documenting family descendancy.

Finnegan, Ruth. *Oral Literature in Africa.* New York: Oxford University Press, 1972.

Author believes study of African oral literature is relevant for any study of Africa.

Fry, Amelis R. "Nine Commandments of Oral History." *Journal of Oral History.* 3(1968): 63-73.

Practical points on the practice of oral history.

Hoopes, James. *Oral History: An Introduction for Students.* Chapel Hill, N.C.: University of North Carolina Press, 1979.

Discusses the relationship of oral history to history.

In Small Things Forgotten. New York: Doubleday, 1977.

Includes an oral history investigation of a free black community in Massachusetts. Significant findings of objects probably made in West Africa and grouping of houses reflect the resident's African heritage.

Index to the American Slave. Edited by Donald Jacobs. Westport, Conn.: Greenwood Press, 1981. [Contributions in Afro-American and African Studies, No. 65].

Indian Pioneer History. An Oral History Collection in the Oklahoma Historical Society Collection. Oklahoma City, Okla.

Recollections of early Oklahoma settlers and pioneers including Afro-Americans.

Meckler, Alan and Ruth Mullin, compilers. *Oral History Collections*. New York: R.R. Bowker Co., 1975.

Comprehensive source for locating oral history transcriptions.

Montell, William Conrad. *The Saga of Coe Ridge: A Study in Oral History*. Knoxville, Tenn.: University Press, 1970.

Good example of the use of oral history to reconstruct historical events in the absence of written records.

Nichols, Charles Harold. *Many Thousands Gone: The Ex-Slaves' account of Their Bondage and Freedom*. Bloomington, Ind.: University Press, 1969.

Excellent oral history source.

"Oral Tradition: Deep Well of African History." *United Nations Monthly Chronicle*, 19(July 1982): 85-86.

Shaw, Nate. *All God's Dangers: The Life of Nate Shaw*. Edited by Theodore Rosengarten. New York: Alfred A. Knopf, 1974.

An oral account of the life of a strong, powerful rural southern black man told by himself.

Thompson, Paul. *The Voice of the Past: Oral History*. New York: Oxford University Press, 1978.

Establishes that oral history is a proper research technique.

Towle, W. Wilder. *The Oral History of James Nunn, A Unique North Carolinian, 1882-1975*. Chapel Hill, N.C.: The Historical Society, 1977.

Interviews with a long-time, highly respected Orange County, North Carolina, resident.

Turner, Lorenzo Dow. *Africanism in the Gullah Dialect*. Chicago: University of Chicago Press, 1949.

The distinctly African speech form has survived and with it much of African languages and meanings.

Tyler, Ronnie C., and Lawrence R. Murphy, editors. *The Slave Narratives of Texas*. Austin, Tex.: Encina Press, 1974.

Vansina, Jan. *Oral Tradition: A Study in Historical Methodology*. London: Routledge and Kegan Paul.

The author is also known for his knowledge of Africa and African languages.

PART II

PRIVATE RESOURCES

A. SITES AND LOCATIONS
B. CHURCHES
    1. General References
    2. Specific Sources
C. CEMETERIES AND BURIAL GROUNDS
D. MANUSCRIPTS
    1. Guides and General References
    2. Papers and Collections
    3. Plantation Records
E. BIBLES
F. PHOTOGRAPHS
G. SOCIETIES AND ORGANIZATIONS
H. EDUCATION INSTITUTIONS-PRIVATE
I. MISCELLANEOUS SOURCES
    1. Clipping Files
    2. Funeral Programs
    3. Insurance Records
    4. Marriage Programs
    5. Medical Records
    6. Scrapbooks
    7. Maps

The social and legal structures in America prior to 1865 excluded the majority of Afro-Americans from printed public documents that would have identified them as individuals. Thus, researchers must put more reliance on oral history and private sources than may be true of genealogy research for some other national and ethnic groups. While public records after 1865 such as censuses of population, tax rolls, voter registration lists, and farm and farm workers data will include Afro-Americans, research on earlier individuals and families will more often require the use of private collections and holdings of families and individuals and estate or manuscript collections of institutions or organizations. Resources identified in this section illustrate the variety of materials and sources found largely in the private domain that are often indispensable in general as well as specific Afro-American genealogy research.

A. SITES AND LOCATIONS

All These Things Are Us (videotape) Moncure, N.C.: 1979.

This videotape consists of scenes of the all-black reconstruction town of Moncure, North Carolina, and interviews with descendants of early settlers. (See Oral History section for further details.)

Ascher, Robert. "How to Build a Time Capsule." *Journal of Popular Culture*, 8: 241-253.

Report of the 1954 excavation of a Colonial log cabin near Wilmington (Delaware) which was last occupied by a black man.

Ascher, Robert and Charles Fairbanks. "Excavation of a Slave Cabin: in Georgia, U.S.A." *Historical Archaeology*, 5(1971): 3-17.

Attempts to discover and convey a sense of daily life as it may have been expressed by cabin occupants constitute this scholarly presentation.

Bingham, Alfred M. "Squatter Settlements of Freed Slaves in New England." *Connecticut Historical Society Bulletin*, 41(July 1976): 65-68.

Bower, Beth Anne. "Historical Archaeology Investigations: A Methodology for Developing Insights into Colonial Early American Life." *Technology and Conservation*, 2(3): 32-37.

Discusses the archaeological excavations accompanying the restoration of an 1806 church built for the black community.

Cass County, Michigan. Calvin Township. Papers on the history of the black settlement in Calvin Township, Cass County, Michigan, 1939. (BeHLUM)

Combes, John D. *Ethnography, Archaeology and Burial Practices among Coastal South Carolina Blacks*. Institute of Archaeology and Anthropology, Conference on Historical Sites. Archaeology Papers. 7: 52-61. Columbia, S.C.: University of South Carolina, 1972.

Negros of Thomas Price of Wake Co.
and descendants who remained with the
Blake and Mial Family

Negros Inherited by Thomas Price, Jr., from his father	Individual Who Acquired Ownership on Thomas Price's Death

Washington Price moved to Miss.
Needham Price
Scheherazade Mial
Washington Price
Scheherazade Mial

- Isaac
- Dinah
  - Ephrim b May 1797
- Rose
  - Chaney (China) b 27 Feb 1793 d 13 Nov 1846
    - Ann (Anaca) b Dec 1812 d 20 Apr 1855
      - Prince b 11 Dec 1833 d 19 Feb 1855
      - Eveline b 10 Mar 1835
      - Hester Ann b 21 Dec 1836
      - Emma 10 Aug 1839
      - Tabitha b 6 Oct 1842
      - Shade b 3 June 1843 d 26 Jun 1853
      - Delsey b 19 Feb 1845
      - Chaney b 15 Dec 1846
      - Son b 16 Dec 1849 d before 1860
    - Meekins b Nov 1814
    - Nelson b Dec 1816
    - Calvin b 16 Oct 1818
    - Western b Sep 1820
  - Lucy b Jun 1797 — Bennett T. Blake
    - Cherry b May 1824
      - Olive b 18 Apr 1841
      - Sally b 22 Sep 1842
      - Cornelia b 19 Feb 1845
      - Harman b 23 Sep 1847
      - Dicer b 19 Aug 1849
      - Independence b 4 July 1852
      - Fabeous b 24 Sept 1857
    - Allen b Mar 1828
    - Aquilla b Oct 1829 d 17 Aug 1860
      - Arramenta b 16 Nov 1857 d 27 Aug 1859
      - Nicey b 11 Mar 1859
      - Edward b 27 May 1860
  - Watt b 9 Apr 1805 d 26 Sept 1891 — Scheherazade Mial

Family lineage constructed from Private sources.

Crockett, Norman L. *Black Towns.* Lawrence, Kan.: Regents Press of Kansas, 1979.

Five all-black towns established in the late nineteenth century are the focus of this study.

Deetz, James. "Black Settlement at Plymouth." *Archaeology*, 29: 207.

Summary of the excavation results at Parting Ways, a small community located near Plymouth, Massachusetts, granted to four freed slaves after their service in the Continental Army during the American Revolution. Archaeological evidence showed that these men retained much of their African cultural background.

Fairbanks, Charles H. *The Kingsley Slave Cabins in Duval County, Florida, 1968.* Institute of Archaeology and Anthropology. Conference on Historical Sites. Archaeology Papers, 7:62-93. Columbia, S.C.: University of South Carolina, 1972.

An archaeological report on the excavation of a slave cabin and a foreman's cabin.

Fitzgerald, Ruth Coder. *A Different Story: A Black History of Fredericksburg, Stafford and Spotsylvania, Virginia.* Frederickson, Va.: Fitzgerald/Unicorn, 1984.

Contains hundreds of family names, many of which can still be found in the area. Presents new information about the black communities of the area.

Jackson, Susan. "Current Research: Southeast." *Society for Historical Archaeology Newsletter*, 10, 2 (1977): 21-24.

Briefly describes the excavation undertaken by Dr. Thomas Loftfield of the University of North Carolina at Wilmington in preparation for the restoration of the slave quarters.

Kelso, William M. *The Colonial Silent Majority: Tenant, Servant, and Slave Settlement Sites at Kingsmill, Virginia.* Paper delivered at the American Anthropological Association. 75th Annual Meeting. Washington, D.C.: 1965.

McFarlane, Suzanne S. *The Ethnohistory of a Slave Community: The Couper Plantation Site.* M.A. Thesis. University of Florida, Gainesville.

McGee, Betty. *Early Black Settlements in Ohio*. Dayton, Ohio: MUCGH Conference, February 13, 1983. (45-min. cassette tape) (ALPLI)

Mobley, Joe A. *James City: A Black Community in North Carolina, 1863-1900*. Raleigh, N.C.: North Carolina State Archives, 1981.

James City was established on the banks of the Trent River near New Bern, North Carolina, during the Civil War and served as a haven for black refugees from the Confederate states.

Montell, William Lynwood. *Folk History of the Coe Ridge Negro Colony*. Ann Arbor: Mich. University Micro Films, 1973.

A doctoral dissertation of oral history of a small black colony in Cumberland County, Kentucky.

Montgomery, Thomas. Letters, 1862-67. (MnHS)

Includes information on a black farming community in St. Peter Land District, Minnesota.

North Fork, Oklahoma. Fort Worth Archives Microfilm 7RA12-2, Abstracted from the 1890 Census (OkHS)

North Fork is the only "colored" town on the 1890 Census record. 1895 Census lists three "colored towns": Arkansas, Canadian, and North Fork. The 1896 "Colbert" roll of Creek (Indians) includes rolls for three colored towns: Arkansas, Canadian, and Concharty.

Pease, William H., and Jane H. Pease. "Organized Negro Communities: A North American Experiment." *Journal of Negro History, XLVIII* (No. I, January 1962): 19-34.

Rose, Harold M. "The All-Negro Town: Its Evolution and Function." *Geographical Review*. 55(July 1965): 362-381.

Socioeconomic study of all-Negro towns in the United States.

Schuyler, Robert L. *Sandy Grove: Archaeological Sampling in a Black Community in Metropolitan New York*. Institute of Archaeology and Anthropology. Conference on Historic Sites. Archaeological Papers, 7:13-52. Columbia, South Carolina: University of South Carolina, 1972.

Several house foundation and trash deposit excavations

and cemetery studies are detailed in this lengthy summary of the archaeological investigation of a black oystermen's community on Staten Island.

Shenkel, J. Richard and Jack Hudson. *Historic Archaeology in New Orleans*. The Institute of Archaeology and Anthropology. Conference on Historical Sites. Archaeological papers, 6:4044. Columbia, S.C.: University of South Carolina, 1971.

Focuses on the excavations in the slave quarters area of the National Trust property.

Steward, William, and Theopphilus Gould Steward. *Gouldtown, a Very Remarkable Settlement of Ancient Date*. Philadelphia: J.B. Lippincott Co., 1913.

A town in existence today whose inhabitants include descendants of Elizabeth Fenwick who married a black man named Adam.

Taylor, Quintard. "The Emergence of Black Communities in the Pacific Northwest, 1865-1910." *Journal of Negro History*, 64 (Fall 1969): 342-51.

Documentation includes use of black newspapers, church records, and biographical materials.

B. CHURCHES

1. General References

Bacob, Samuel Williams, ed. *Who's Who Among Colored Baptists of the United States*. Kansas City, Mo.: Franklin Hudson Publ., 1913.

Bradley, David H. *A History of the A.M.E.Z. Church*. Nashville, Tenn.: Parthson Press, 1956.

Bragg, George. *Afro-American Churchwork and Workers*. Baltimore: The Author, 1904.

Frazier, E. Franklin. *The Negro Church in America* and C. Eric Lincoln, *The Black Church since Frazier*. New York: Schocken Books, 1963. [Sourcebook in Negro History].

Historical Reference Survey of Virginia. *Inventory of the Church Archives of Virginia*. *Negro Baptist*

Churches in Richmond. Richmond, Va.: The Historical Records Survey, 1940.

Historical Sketch of the Freedmen's Mission of the Presbyterian Church, 1862-1904. Knoxville, Tenn.: Presbyterian Church, 1904.

Work of the denomination in helping blacks into the twentieth century.

Kirkman, E. Kay. *A Survey of American Church Records.* Salt Lake City, Utah: Deseret Book Co., 1971.

Location of American church records including lists of members, some of whom are black.

Koger, Azzie Briscoe. *History of Negro Baptists of Maryland.* Baltimore: Clarke Press, 1942.

Nelsen, Hart M., Raytha L. Yokley, and Anne Nelsen. *The Black Church in America.* New York: Basic Books, Inc., 1971.

Williams, Ethel L. *Biographical Directory of Negro Ministers.* Metuchen, N.J.: Scarecrow Press, 1965. 1965.

Reference book on the American Negro and the clergy including biographical data and a bibliography on suggested sources for further information on ministers, churches, and denominations.

———. *Biographical Directory of Negro Ministers.* 3rd ed. Boston: G.K. Hall, 1975.

2. Specific Sources

African Methodist Episcopal Church, Detroit, Michigan. Slides. Third-generation copies of the African Methodist Episcopal Church, Detroit, c. 1935. (BeHLUM)

Includes views of the church, its officials, and congregation. Slides taken from originals and recopied in 1964 and 1983.

Amistad Research Center. New Orleans, Louisiana. Collections:
American and Foreign Anti-Slavery Society, Minutes.
American Home Missionary Society, Archives.
American Missionary Association, Archives.

Catholic Committee of the South.
Methodist Episcopal Church Records.

Baptist Historical Collection. Furman University Library, Greenville, South Carolina.

Includes microfilm copies of records of individual churches in the nineteenth century concerning slave membership.

Bethel A.M.E.Z. Church, Detroit, 1911-1969. (BrHCDPL)

Baptisms, marriages, and membership records are retained on microfilm.

Bethel African Methodist Episcopal Church, South Carolina, 1974. Music. (SCHS)

Services at Lovely Hill Baptist church with a sermon recorded by Rev. Deas are included as well as services at New Hope AMEZ church and others.

Catholic Church, Halifax, Nova Scotia. Parish Registers for Colored People, 1827-1835.

Records of baptisms, marriages, and burials of members.

Center for Research Libraries, Chicago, Illinois. Douglass Collection.

Collection contains a number of studies concerned with black churches in changing neighborhoods.

Concordia Historical Institute of Missouri, St. Louis.

This agency maintains records of the Lutheran Church.

Congregational Church, Windham, Connecticut. Records, 1700-1851. (CnHS)

History of the church was written in Hartford in 1943. Records include references to blacks.

Filson Club, Louisville, Kentucky.

Collection includes records of Beech Creek Baptist Church, Shelby, Kentucky, 1825-1840; Buffalo Lick Baptist Church, 1805-1838; Christenburg Baptist Church, 1810-1875.

Glassboro State College, Glassboro, New Jersey. Quaker Collection.

Collection includes Salem County manumissions for 1777.

Michigan University Library, Ann Arbor. American Home Missionary Society. Records.

Mississippi State University, Mitchell Memorial Library, State College.
Church Records:
Baptist Church Records, 1819-1957.
Church of Christ Records, 1900-1957.
Episcopal Church Records, 1848-1888.
Methodist Church Records, 1833-1957.
Presbyterian Church Records, 1823-1885.
Primitive Baptist Church Records, 1819-1957.

Records include church rolls, baptisms, marriages, funerals and registers of black and white members.

Missouri State Historical Society.
Negro Churches Collection:
African Methodist Episcopal Church Records, 1901--
Baptist Church Records, 1909--
Christian Church of Missouri Annual Meeting Records, 1889, 1900, 1903 and 1904.

Mother HUMP Church, Wilmington, Delaware.
Records 1874-1969. (DelHS)

Records are of business and other church activities.

New York (State). Church and Cemetery Records.
See: Section on CEMETERIES.

North Carolina State Archives, Raleigh, N.C.
Collection includes:
Episcopal Church Records, 1850-1927.
Christian Church Records, 1939-1962.

Ohio Historical Society.
Collection includes:
AMEZ Church Records for Bishops.
Allen's Chapel Church Records, 1854.
Free Will Baptist Church Records, 1819-1916.

St. Francis of Xavier Parish, Louisiana.
Records, 1749-1838. (IndHS)

Records on blacks in this collection date from 1753.

St. Louis Church, New Orleans, Louisiana. Archives.

Marriage registers of Negroes and mulattoes date from 1730.

St. Matthews Episcopal Church, Detroit, Michigan,
Records, 1894-1973. (BrHCDPL)

Confirmation, baptism, death, and marriage records comprise the collection.

Second Baptist Church, Detroit, Michigan, 1935-1979.
(BrHCDPL)

Marriage and death records are on microfilm.

Smith, Charles Spencer, 1852-1923. Papers, 1875-1923.

Smith was a teacher and Bishop of the AMEZ church. Collection contains correspondence, speeches, and printed material relating to settlement of Liberia by American blacks, education of blacks, and related topics.

South Carolina Episcopal Church. Records, 1694-1942.
(SCHS)

Church registers have some references to blacks.

Trinity Methodist Episcopal Church, Charleston, South Carolina.
Roll Book, 1821-1868. (SCHS)
Book C; List of Negro members.

Tennessee State Library and Archives, Nashville.
Collection includes:
Baptist. Mill Creek Baptist Church, Davidson County, Tennessee. 1794-1814.
A list of black membership is included.
Catholic. St. Joseph Catholic Mission, Jackson (Madison County), Tennessee.
Records are of missions established for blacks.
Disciples of Christ. Collection of black churchmen.
Methodist Episcopal Church.
Minutes, 1866-1888; 1905-1925. Minutes of both black and white church conferences.

United Church of Christ, New Orleans, Louisiana. Records of 1872-1984. (AmRC)

Central records of the United Church of Christ.

United Methodist Church, Jeffersonville, Indiana. 1866-1981. (IndSL)

History of Wesley United Methodist Church which was founded by slaves.

Wilberforce University Library, Xenia, Ohio.
Collection includes:
American Missionary Society, Papers.
AMEZ Church, Records of former Bishops.
Society of Friends, Papers.

C. CEMETERIES AND BURIAL GROUNDS

Private cemeteries and burial grounds include family cemeteries on private property, church cemeteries, and cemeteries owned by private concerns such as funeral directors, burial associations, and insurance companies. Prior to 1865 most blacks in slaveholding states were interred in *burial grounds*. Some are known to be buried in family lots of slave holders. Family papers may reveal such instances. Blacks, both slave and free, are buried in church cemeteries where they were members. Still others are buried in public cemeteries in many cities.

Some local historical and genealogical societies have undertaken to survey cemeteries and burial grounds in specific states and communities. Librarians and genealogists may survey these organizations to determine if unpublished projects and findings on cemeteries are available. North Carolina is one of the states that participated in the United States Works Projects Administration of the 1930s that indexed tombstone inscriptions in cemeteries throughout the state.

The variety of types of cemeteries in America poses problems for the genealogist and especially the black researcher. Local government officials, church officials, funeral directors, early residents of a community, and family papers are useful sources in locating and identifying cemeteries.

Alabama Agricultural and Mechanical State University, Huntsville. Archives.

Archives include records of concrete slabs unearthed on former Kinkaid plantation during building excavation at the University. Burials of former slaves date 1831-1877.

Allowance of Meat arranged for 1856.

√ George, Wilsey. Isaac, Aaron . 2 2½ . 2½ — 5½ pounds 11½
√ Willie, Anny. Margaret. Mittie Richmond . . — 6½ 9
√ Moses. Jamelia. Julia Alexander Rhody . . — 6½
√ Ben. Lizzy. Dempsy, Mahala. Louisa Carnell . . — 7½
√ Martin. Sallie. Louis. Hector. Ambrose. . . . — 8½
Henry . — 3½
Joshua . . . — 2.
Nathaniel . . . . — 3½
Fortune . . . . — 3½
Lyttle . . . . — 3½
Gaston . . . . . — 3½
√ Isom. Caroline. Allen . . . — 4½
Hasa . . . . . . — 3½
√ Solomon. Esther Mary Ann . . . — 6½
Jim Renton . . . . — ~~5½~~ 6
Lee . . . . — 3½
Joseph . . . . — ~~3½~~
~~Rodric~~ . Wiley 3½ . — ~~2½~~
Bedford . Roberts Wiley 2½ . — 2½
Stuford . . . . — 2½
Amp~~hes~~ . . . . — 2½
√ Emily. Jesse, Diana, Silvy & her infant Harry.

THIS COPY OF A PAGE TAKEN FROM THE BLOUNT FAMILY SLAVE RATION BOOK REVEALS FAMILY GROUPS. MALES NAMES APPEAR AT THE BEGINNING OF MOST OF THE FAMILY GROUPS.
NOTE: "Philemon (and) Hannah (and) 2 small children"

"Cemetery Only Evidence of Extinct Community." *Times Bulletin*, Van Wert, Ohio. Wednesday, October 4, 1978: 14. (ALPLI)

Includes a list of people buried in the colored cemetery, East Wren Cemetery.

Cemetery Records of Forsyth County, North Carolina. Compiled by Donald W. Staley; editor, Ann E. Sheek, and Hazel R. Hartmen, Winston-Salem, N.C.: Hunter Publishing Co., 1972-1978. 5 v.

This work includes "collected data from every tombstone that could be found in the county." Cemeteries are largely church and family.

Daughters of the American Revolution. Guilford Battle Chapter, Greensboro, North Carolina. *Bible, Cemetery and Family Records, Deeds/Wills.* Greensboro, N.C.: 1957.

Abstracts of wills include names of slaves owned and willed.

Franklin County Historical Society. *Cemetery Records of Franklin County, Tennessee.* Compiled by the Society, Winchester, Tenn.: 1984.

This valuable resource includes maps with locations of burial grounds and cemeteries labeled "colored."

Greenwood Cemetery, Nashville, Tennessee.

Maintained by a religious organization, this cemetery has the remains of some of the city's leading figures and personalities in black history. Included are such names as Charles S. Johnson and George Hubbard (Hubbard Hospital of Meharry Medical College).

Mount Olive Cemetery, Mother HUMP Church, Wilmington, Delaware, 1843-1937. (DelHS)

Five burials are recorded during the period, 1818-1903.

National Funeral Directors and Morticians Association, Chicago, Illinois.

Names and locations of black funeral directors and embalmers throughout the United States and some Caribbean nations. Potential sources of information on burials and burial places.

New York (State) Library, Albany. Church and Cemetery Records.

The State Library of New York has an extensive collection of church (protestant only) and cemetery records predating 1880 when the state did not keep vital records. The collection contains published records, registers deposited in the State Library, and others compiled by the New York State Chapters of Daughters of the American Revolution.

North Carolina, Department of Archives and History, Raleigh. Index to Tombstones.

The Archives maintains an index to tombstones found in cemeteries in all counties in North Carolina. The project was undertaken by personnel provided by the Works Projects Administration in the 1930s.

Ohio Cemetery Records Extracted from the 'Old Northwest Genealogical Quarterly.' Baltimore: Genealogical Publishing Co., 1984.

Publication includes a list of names of persons interred in the Africa Graveyard, Orange Township, Delaware County, Ohio.

Orton Plantation, Wilmington, North Carolina. Burial Ground.

This plantation maintained a burial ground (ca. 1725-1976) for slaves and descendants of former slaves. Afro-Americans continued to bury their dead at this site until 1976. Descendants of former slaves still work on the plantation.

Pritchard, Katharine A. *Ancient Burying Grounds of the Town of Waterbury, Connecticut*. New Haven, Conn.: 1917.

United States Works Projects Administration. *Negro Bibles and Cemetery Records: Tennessee*. Nashville; WPA. Tennessee Historical Records Survey, 1941.

Private and public sources listed.

D. MANUSCRIPTS

1. Guides and General References

Amistad Research Center, New Orleans, Louisiana. Anti-Slavery Collection.

Collection contains letters of American Missionary Society in opposition to slavery; bills of sale and free papers.

Benton, Arthur J. *A Guide to the Manuscript Collections of the New York Historical Society.* Westport, Conn.: Greenwood Press, 1972.

Boston Public Library. Anti-Slavery Collection, 1820-1900.

Collection includes account books, manuscripts, and letters relating to freedmen's schools, slavery in the West Indies, and the Mather family papers.

Connecticut Historical Society. Slavery Documents of Connecticut, 1751-1851.

Collection includes bills of sale and other documents of slavery on microfilm.

Duke University. Perkins Library. *Guide to the Manuscript Collections in the Duke University Library.* Prepared by Nannie M. Tilly and Noma Lee Goodman. Durham, N.C.: Duke University Press, 1947.

An out-of-print guide to a massive amount of records including private family papers, diaries, bills of sale, and names of free blacks.

Fisk University Library, Nashville, Tennessee. Negro Collection.

This collection includes diaries and letters, certificates of freedom, and slave labor contracts. Many items formerly maintained in this collection have been removed to the Amistad Research Center, New Orleans, La.

Guide to Manuscript Collections and Institutional Records in Ohio. Edited by David R. Larson. Columbus, Ohio: Society of Ohio Archivists, 1974.

Guide to Manuscript Sources for the History of Latin America and the Caribbean in the British Isles. Edited by Peter Walne. London: Oxford University, 1973.

Includes an abundance of records relevant to black genealogy that are grouped in volumes by date.

Lantz, Andrea D. *A Guide to Manuscripts at the Ohio Historical Society.* Columbus: Ohio Historical Society, 1972.

McDonough, John. "Manuscript Resources for the Study of Negro Life and History." *Quarterly Journal of the Library of Congress*, 26, 3(July 1969): 126-48.

Maryland Historical Society. *The Manuscript Collection of the Maryland Historical Society.* Compiled by Avril J. Pedley. Baltimore, 1968.

Guide to family papers including slave records.

National Union Catalog of Manuscripts Collection: Based on Reports from American Repositories of Manuscripts. Ann Arbor, Mich.: J.W. Edwards, 1951-61.

Entries include descriptions of the manuscript collection cited and availability of collection on microfilm.

New Orleans Public Library. Manuscripts - Archives Collection. Papers, ca. 1750-.

Collection contains documents regarding New Orleans ordinances and suits brought against free blacks from before the Civil War.

North Carolina. Department of Archives and History. Slave Collection, 1748-1856.

Collection of original and photocopied documents relating to slavery in North Carolina. Includes deeds of gift and bills of sale; permission to marry, insurrection in Bertie County (1802), and reimbursement for executed slaves, etc.

North Carolina University, Wilson Library, Chapel Hill. Southern Historical collection. *The Southern Historical Collection: A Guide to Manuscripts* by Susan Sokol Blosser and Clyde Norman Wilson, Jr. Chapel Hill, N.C.: 1970.

Ohio State Historical Society, Columbus. Miscellaneous Documents Collection, 1800-60.

Collection includes slave receipts and manumission papers.

Oklahoma Department of Libraries. *Guide to Oklahoma Manuscripts, Maps and Newspapers on Microfilm in the Oklahoma Department of Libraries.* Compiled and edited by Robert L. Clark, Jr., Oklahoma City: 1970.

Scott, Olivia Barbara. *A Classified Sociological Source Bibliography of Periodical and Manuscript Materials on the Negro in Atlanta, Georgia.* Wooster, Ohio: Bell and Howell Black Culture Collection, #571-1, 1984.

South Carolina Historical Society. *Manuscript Guide*, by David Moltke-Hansen and Sally Dasher. Charleston: The Society, 1979.

Tennessee State Library and Archives. *Negro Materials in the Manuscript Section.* Nashville: Tennessee State Library and Archives, 1969.

Trevor Arnett Library. Atlanta University, Georgia. *Guide to Manuscripts and Archives in the Negro Collection of Trevor Arnett Library.* Atlanta University, Georgia: 1971.

West Virginia. University. West Virginia Collection. *Guide to Manuscripts and Archives in the West Virginia Collection.* Compiled by James W. Hess. Morgantown, W. Va.: University Library, 1974.

2. Papers and Collections

Atwood, Rufus B.
Papers. (KeCF)

Papers and memoirs of former President of Kentucky

State College at Frankfort.

Bailey Everett Hoskins.
Family Papers, 1839-1954. (MnHS)

Boxes of materials on black education in the state are included in this collection.

Barbot Family.
Papers, 1795-1949. (SCHS)

Discusses Cuban holdings of Jean Pierre Esnard and Antoine Barbot; purchase of slaves and properties in Charleston County (SC) by A. Barbot.

Bennett, John, 1865-1956.
Papers. ca. 1865-1960. (SCHS)

This collection includes family correspondence, papers of the slave trade, etc.; the Gullah people, black music and folklore.

Brice (Carol) Papers (John Carol, Lolita, Eugene, Jonathan, and Charlotte Hawkins Brown), 1905-1984. (AmRC)

Papers of Brice brothers and sisters and Guion Bluford, astronaut son of Lolita, are included in collection.

Brown, Godfrey, 1822-1880.
Papers. (AmRC)

Brown descendants' collection contains freedom papers of Godfrey Brown and items by other members of the family including contemporary descendants.

Cullen (Countee, Ida, Frederick, Caroline).
Papers. (AmRC)

Countee Cullen was a leading writer during the Harlem Renaissance.

Dixon, Henry.
Family Papers. (AmRC)

Miscellanea of Henry, his wife, Cecelia, and father, George. Includes real estate tax receipts issued to successive generations for the same property.

Dobbs, John W.
Family Papers. (AmRC)

Dobbs, John (Irene), five daughters; grandchildren; great-grandchildren. John was a fraternal leader and politician in Atlanta, Ga.; children: Mattiwilda, vocalist; former mayor Maynard (Atlanta); Josephine (Dobbs) Clement of Durham, elected official.

Embree, Lucius C., 1813-1830.
Family Papers. (IndSL)

Includes legal papers, wills, bills of sale, indentured paper of James Tharp and letter concerning free papers of David Prossner of Madison, Indiana. (Family links also include Stevens, Gay, and Shannon; Tharp and Prossner are black.)

Gregg, Phineas, 1800-
Papers, 1849-1882. (BeHLUM)

Papers of Phineas Gregg, Justice of the Peace of Cass County, Michigan. Includes medical account book, records of marriages, 1850-1869, and of the Sanders Colony of blacks; deeds to property and miscellanea.

Jones, Samuel
Papers, 1760-1793.

Collection includes list of slaves who were manumitted in 1779.

Lasselle, Charles B. 1816-1819.
Family Papers. (IndSL)

Contains legal papers including deeds and papers of indenture of servitude. Family names in collection include Lasselle, LaPlante, Posey, Bosseron, Hale, Cunningham, residents or past residents of Kentucky and Tennessee.

Palmer, William Pendleton.
Collection, 1861-1927. (WRHSC)

Letters on plantation life and the underground railroad; military records and lists of casualties of black regiments in the South.

Patterson (Zella)
Collection on the history of Langston University. (OkHS)

Simonton, Charles H.
Papers, 1854-1902. (SCHS)

Charleston attorney, trustee of Mrs. Julia M. Graves. Papers include mortgages and conveyances of slaves and lands.

Smith, Daniel Elliott Huger, 1846-1932.
Papers, 1716-1922. (SCHS)

Memoranda dated 1836 on Negroes on the estate of John E. Farr.

Sublette Family.
Papers, 1848-1854. (MoHS)

Includes transactions with B.M. Lauch, slave trader and documents on runaway slaves.

Whitridge, Joshua Barker, 1789-1865.
Papers, 1806-1865. (SCHS)

Slavery, plantation life, work among Civil War refugees and statistics of Rose Bank Plantation.

Winn Family.
Papers, 1788-1925 (DuPL)

Includes journals, account books, and records of births and deaths of slaves.

Young, Whitney More, Sr.
Papers. (KeCF)

Contains letters and related papers of noted public figure and father of Urban League director.

3. Plantation Records

Allston, Robert F.W., 1801-1864.
Plantation Book, 1846-1852. (SCHS)

Nightingale Hall, Georgetown County Plantation Book contains accounts kept with slaves and slave birth and death records; James Kelly, overseer.

Bacot, Huger
Papers, 1752-1945. (SCHS)

Charleston-born historian, educator, journalist. Papers include receipts for rice sales and for slaves in the workhouse in Charleston; Negro disturbance.

Ball, John, 1782-1834.
Plantation Account Book, 1812-1834. (SCHS)

Occasional accounts with slaves and free blacks.

"Picture postcards" were popular around the turn of the century. This postcard is a photograph developed at the Violet Studio, Nashville Arcade, Tennessee. The subject is Lena Lane Osteen. The names "James Brown and 'Watty' Brown" appear on the face of the postcard.

Ball, John.
Plantation Records, 1738-1895. (SCHS)

Records of clothing and blankets given to Negroes at Comingtee Stake, Kensington and Midway Plantations.

Barker, Sanford William, 1807-1891.
Plantation Records, 1841-1867. (SCHS)

Register of Negroes at Mulberry plantation.

Barnwell, Rev. William Hazzard Wigg, d. 1863.
Plantation Book, 1859. (SCHS)

List of Negroes and their ages in 1866 and clothes of Negroes for 1847-1861.

Belin, Allard, Sr.
Plantation Records, 1792-1798. (SCHS)

Contains notes on runaway slaves and plantation expenses; records of work, notes on slaves and lists of blankets given to Negroes.

Black, George, B. 1814.
Papers, 1829-1887. (SCHS)

Includes bills of sale of slaves.

Chaplin, Thomas, 1822-1890.
Plantation Journal, 1845-1886. (SCHS)

Daily entries, rental of, and treatment of slaves are included in the journal.

Cheves, Langdon I., 1776-1857.
Plantation Papers, 1736-1863. (SCHS)

Plantation Papers, 1837-1861, reference to Langsyne Plantation in Calhoun County, S.C., etc.

Coffin, Thomas Ashton, 1795-1863.
Plantation Records, 1800-1813. (SCHS)

Records of Coffin Point Plantation, Beaufort, S.C.: Lists of blankets given to slaves; plantation accounts, daily entries for work done on the plantation; birth and sicknesses of Negroes, 1813.

Dulles Family.
Plantation Book, 1797-1860. (SCHS)

Record of Good Hope Plantation, Orangeburg County,

S.C. List of Negroes sold to Augustus W. Smith; register of slave births and deaths, 1797-1831. This plantation is a subject of study in Gutman's *The Black Family in Slavery and Freedom: 1750-1925.*

Gaillard, Peter, Sr., 1757-1833.
Plantation Account and Memoranda, 1783-1832. (SCHS)

Lists of births and deaths of Negroes from 1786.

Gaillard Family.
Plantation Book, 1825-1847. (SCHS)

Contains lists of Negroes with register of births, deaths, and marriages, reference to Mrs. H.P. Gaillard, J. Gaillard, L.C. and Thomas Gaillard.

Gourdin, P.
Plantation Records, 1847. (SCHS)

List of Negroes and their ages in 1866 and clothes issued in 1847-1861.

Griffin, Lucille, editor. "The Plantation Book of Brookdale Farm, Amite County, Mississippi, 1856-1857." *Journal of Mississippi History*, 7(1945): 23-31.

Harry, Elias, d. 1834.
Estate Account Book, 1837-1864. (SCHS)

Contains accounts of rice and lists of Negroes on Newland, Midland.

Jackson, Andrew, II
Account Books, 1845-77. (TeSL)

Includes purhase, sale, birth, marriage, and deaths of slaves of Hermitage.

Jefferson, Thomas. *Thomas Jefferson's Farm Book.* Edited by Edwin Morris Betts. Princeton, N.J.: Princeton University Press, 1953.

Jenkins, Rev., Mr., 1744-1821.
Memorandum Book, 1773-1782. (SCHS)

List of Negroes delivered by order of General Henry Clinton.

Leak and Wall Family.
Papers, 1785-1897. (SoHCUNC)

Collection includes miscellaneous farming records and lists of Negroes.

Mississippi Department of Archives and Plantation History Records, 1818-65.

Miscellaneous documents pertaining to Nanechehaw, Assentine, and Nailer plantations. Also materials on Negroes, cotton picking, and family history.

Andrew McCollam Company, Red River Sanding, La.
Account Book, 1838-63. (SoHCUNC)

Includes lists of names of over 100 black persons who were hired out for services.

Manumission Records (Photostats) (SoHCUNC)

Expense account for group of black persons being conveyed from Perquimans County, North Carolina, including names of the individuals.

Multenberger, Christian, 1764-1829.
Account Book. (SoHCUNC)

Memorandum book on rental of houses and slaves in Louisiana.

"A Record from an Eighteenth Century Jamaican Estate." *Journal of Negro History*, 59(April 1974): 168-69.

Shipman, S.K. Lincoln County, Kentucky.
Inventory, February 22, 1860. (IndSL)

List of holdings in subject's estate giving names and ages of slaves.

Sparkman, John, 1815-1897.
Plantation Memorandum Book, 1859-1928. (SCHS)

Dirleton, Georgetown County (the Plantation was also known as Richfield.) Lists of births and deaths of Negroes, 1859-1863; measurements of persons for clothing and the names of the individuals, 1859-64.

Ward, John Joshua, 1800-1869.
Account Book, 1831-1869. (SCHS)

Records of Rosedew and Springfield Plantations on

the Waccamaw River, Georgetown County. Contains list of slaves, accounts of sick days, and tools given to individuals. Also accounts with workers after the Civil War.

Webb, Daniel (d. 1850)
Plantation Journal, 1815-1850. (SCHS)

Notes on crops, blankets, and clothing distribution, and births and deaths of blacks on the plantation.

E. BIBLES

Bibles, once owned by most families, are an excellent source of genealogical information. Information found in Bibles includes names of persons, birth and death dates, marriage dates, military service dates, and miscellanea. While many black families prior to 1865 may not have owned and maintained Bible records, many after 1865 did and continue to do so. Many slaveholders' Bibles included names, births, deaths, and marriages of all persons on a property.

Family Bibles are found in collections of estate papers in public and private agencies and in the personal possession of individuals. Data extracted from family Bibles also appear in printed monographs and typewritten copies. Local genealogical societies sometimes undertake projects to collate family Bibles, and some of these projects are not widely known. A survey of local genealogical society holdings could prove valuable.

Daughters of the American Revolution. Guilford Battle Chapter, Greensboro, North Carolina. *Bible, Cemetery and Family Records, Deed/Wills*. Greensboro, N.C.: 1957.

Includes extracted data from Bibles and excerpts from wills including the names of slaves.

Daughters of the American Revolution, New York (State)
Bible Records, v. 1 - 1924 to present. 192 vols. (NYSL)

Primarily a collection of family Bible records listed by surname in card index in the local history and genealogy area of the library.

Maury County Historical Society. *Maury County Cousins: Bible and Family Records*, compiled by the Society, 1967.

Lists births, marriages, and death dates of Maury County (now Marshall) Tennessee persons. Names of blacks appear in sections of some Bibles, including Dardens, Mortons, and Shutts now residing in Nashville, Tennessee.

(See also Section C of this part for United States Works Projects Administration: Tennessee for note on Bibles.)

F. PHOTOGRAPHS

Photographs have been considered a serious source of study by historians and genealogists only in more recent times. Each family photograph--scene of a homestead location or family or a family member--should be regarded as an original document with potential for valuable information.

Photographs play a special role in Afro-American genealogy. The tracking of ancient physical tribal characteristics can be accomplished through photographs, and these recognized characteristics have been known to bring families and others together. Herbert G. Gutman writing in the introduction to his *Black Family in Slavery and Freedom, 1750-1925* states, "The most important single piece of historical evidence in this book is neither an isolated statistic, historical 'anecdote,' a numerical table, nor a chart. It is the *photograph* that adorns the jacket of this book and serves as its frontispiece." The photograph, taken before the Civil War, is that of a black family on the William Joyner Smith plantation and was entitled by the planter, "Five Generations on Smith's Plantation, Beaufort, South Carolina."

Photographs of clubs and fraternal societies, class pictures, and picture postcards that were popular around the turn of the century are good sources of visual information. Copies of photographs clipped from newspapers, photographs in books, and application photographs required by various agencies for employment are additional sources. Major research libraries as the New York Public Library, Schomburg Collection, have photograph collections. Schatz's *Directory of Afro-American Resources* cites several sources for photograph collections.

Alabama. Agricultural and Normal University.
Huntsville, Archives.
Photograph Collection.

Collection includes photographs relating to campus life, individuals, and campus scenes.

Boley, Oklahoma.
Photographs. (OkHs)

Collection of photographs of Boley, Oklahoma, a predominantly black community.

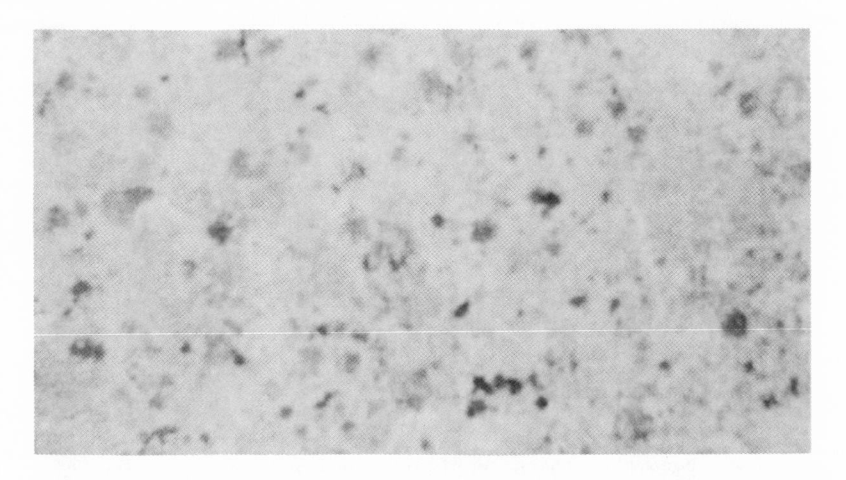

The ravages of time and weather may wear away the lettering on a headstone. The use of a lead pencil and tissue paper aided in revealing that this stone was that of 'Nance L. McCord, . . . 1830 . . .'

Legible markers such as shown above pose little problems in surveying names and dates in cemeteries.

California University, Los Angeles, CAAS.
University of California, Los Angeles, Center for Afro-American Studies.

Historical photograph collection.

Campbell, John Charles and Olive Arnold Dame (Campbell)
Papers. (SoHCUNC)

Collection includes photographs of Afro-Americans in the Appalachian region.

Carmack, Edward Ward
Papers. (SoHCUNC)

Volumes 13 and 14 of this collection include post-bellum photographs of plantation life (ca. 1900) and Afro-Americans of Nashville, Tennessee, and Memphis.

Coker, Robert Ervin, 1876-1967.
Papers, 1906-1956. (SoHCUNC)

Includes photographs depicting social life and customs of Afro-Americans.

Gordy Family of Detroit.
Photographs, ca. 1920-1950. (BeHLUM)

Collection of photographs of the Gordy family and of the Booker T. Washington grocery store.

Indiana. State Board of Charities.
Lantern Slides, ca. 1890s (IndSL)

Includes pictures of black families with some identified by county and surname.

Louis Tendler Elementary School, Detroit, Michigan.
Photographs, Color Slides, and Albums, ca. 1961-81. (BeHLUM)

Collection shows staff, students, and facilities of the largely black elementary school on Detroit's East Side.

Oklahoma Historical Society, Oklahoma City.
Black Oklahomians.

Collection of scattered photographs identifying black Oklahomians.

Penn School, St. Helena Island, South Carolina.
Papers, 1862-1976. (SoHCUNC)

4,200 photographs of Penn School depict black women,

island residents, teachers, and others associated with the school.

Phillips, Charles, 1822-1889.
  Papers, 1839-1960. (SoHCUNC)

Photographs of Afro-American women in Chapel Hill and Rockingham, N.C., and other locations.

Smith, Charles Spencer, 1852-1923.
  Photographs, ca. 1880-1920. (BeHLUM)

Collection contains photographs relating to the life and work of a bishop of the American Methodist Episcopal Church who presided over districts in Canada, South Africa, etc.

Spencer, Chauncey Edward, 1906-.
  Photographs and negatives. (BeHLUM)

Collection contains images relating to life and career of black pilot and charter member of the Negro Pilot's Association. Son of Ann Spencer, well-known poetess of African and Indian descent.

Urban League. Battle Creek (Michigan) Area.
  Photographs, ca. 1965-1974. (BeHLUM)

Photographs reveal activities of the agency including portraits of staff, guest speakers, and citizens active in the Urban League.

Urban League. Grand Rapids (Michigan). Brough Community Association.
  Photographs, 1934-1960. (BeHLUM)

Includes early photographs of the Brough Community Association and its activities, planning groups, committees, and the Women's Guild.

Warmoth, Henry Clay
  Papers. (SoHCUNC)

Large collection of pictures of post-bellum plantation life including Afro-Americans.

G. SOCIETIES AND ORGANIZATIONS.

Beneficial, social, and historical societies and organizations for Afro-Americans began as early as 1787 when the Free African Society was founded by Richard Allen and Absalom Jones in Philadelphia. Fraternal organizations such as the Masons, Eastern Star, and Daughters of Isis have provided social outlet and self-help for Afro-Americans throughout the years. Many local social clubs and, in later years (since the 1920s), Greek-letter organizations at colleges and alumni chapters for graduates have extended social life and self-help in the black community. Many records of early societies and organizations have been lost, yet many records remain available. On the east coast such organizations as the Historical Society of Pennsylvania, Boston University, and the Boston and New York Antiquarian Societies have maintained records on organizations relevant to blacks.

Historically black college and university libraries can be expected to have records of a significant number of societies and organizations that were active or met on the college campus. Public libraries that serve predominantly black communities generally have materials of special interest to local patrons including clipping files, scrapbooks, rosters of organizations, and copies of programs. A growing movement among some public community agencies such as museums that have not heretofore included collections of materials about Afro-Americans is to include items made available by local black citizens. Agencies preserving local history materials such as city and county museums may include significant materials in genealogy research.

American Negro Historical Society, 1790-1901.
Records, 1790-1901. (PeHS)

Includes roll books, lists of black organizations such as the Daughters of Africa Society, Agricultural and Mechanics Association of Pennsylvania and New Jersey, and Negro baseball clubs.

Amistad Research Center, New Orleans, Louisiana.
Records of Organizations.

Records in this collection include various organizations relating to or originated by blacks.

Black, Ford S. *Black's Blue Book: Business and Professional Directory (Chicago)*. Chicago: 1918, 1919, 1921, 1923-1924. (ALPLI)

Brotherhood of Sleeping Car Porters.
Papers, 1925-1969. (CnHS)

Collection contains correspondence, membership records, and related papers of the Brotherhood and its International Ladies Auxiliary.

Catalogue of Black Organizations in Alabama. Compiled by the Collection and Evaluation of Materials about Black Americans Program of the Alabama Center for Higher Education, 1979.

Publication includes a list of 239 black organizations in Alabama including churches, civic, social, professional, and burial associations.

Colored People's Blue Book and Business Directory of Chicago, Illinois. Chicago: Celebrity Printing Co., 1905. (ALPLI)

Colored Welfare League, Ann Arbor, Michigan. Miscellanea, 1930-1944. (BeHLUM)

Collection includes miscellaneous materials of the League and other black community organizations.

Delaware Association for the Moral Improvement and Education of the Colored People of the State, 1866-1909. (DelHS)

Hartford (Connecticut) Freedman Aid Society, 1865-1869. (CnHS)

Collection contains records and photographs.

Indiana Negro Business and Professional Pictorial Guide, 1947-48. (IndSL)

Black business directory for larger Indiana cities giving short biographies of local blacks and histories of benevolent institutions.

Knights and Daughters of Tabor. Official Proceedings of the Knights and Daughters of Tabor International Order of Twelve for the Jurisdiction of Missouri. (MoSHS)

Collection covers proceedings dating from 1894-1926.

Knights of Pythias. Young Men's Pride, Lodge No. 12. (KeSCF)

Miscellaneous collection of memorabilia and names of members.

Ladies Art Club. Greensboro, North Carolina. Roster and Minutes Book, 1916-1927. (GrHM)

Includes the names of local members of the club, some of whom still reside in the city.

Ladies Friends of Faith Benevolent Association.
Minute Books, 1914-1916. (AA&ML)

Lists names of officers and members with addresses in some instances.

Marcus Garvey Universal Negro Improvement Association, 1918-1958.
Papers. (Privately held)

Papers of this organization were held by the Metropolitan Applied Research Center, New York, until it closed in 1976. Records now held by Berenice Simms, New York City.

Negro Association Collection.
Proceedings. (MoHS)

Collection contains records and proceedings for black organizations in Missouri including Knights and Daughters of Tabor, Ancient Order of United Workmen, Order of Fellows, and others.

Negro Directory (Indiana), 1939-1940. (IndSL)

Directory lists business by type covering mostly Terre Haute and Indianapolis areas with some biographical information.

Perry, Thelma D. *History of the American Teachers' Association*. National Education Association, 1975.

History of Black ATA up to its merger with the NEA.

Primrose Arbor. (Black Chapter of the Order of the Gleaners) Calvin Township, Cass County, Michigan. 1906-1917; 1928-1935.
Records. (BeHLUM)

Contains lists of members and financial accounts of organization in Rosana Wilson Collection of Papers.

Societe des Jeunes Amis, 1896-1969.
Minute Books. (AmRC)

United States Department of Commerce. *Negro Trade Associations*. Washington, D.C.: 1936.

Structure and function of Negro trade associations.

H. EDUCATION INSTITUTIONS-PRIVATE

African School Society, Delaware.
Records 1865-1916. (DelHS)

Specific names of blacks are mentioned. Records are primarily of white organizations providing funds for black schools.

Iowa Wesleyan College, Mount Pleasant.
Archives, 1885, 1887, 1891.

Lists names of first black student and graduates.

Leonard Schools of Medicine and Pharmacy, Shaw University, Raleigh, North Carolina.
J.M. Pickell Collection, 1896-1920. (NCAr)

Lists of faculty and students of both schools and the graduates (in medicine, 1886-1902, and pharmacy, 1893-1902). Seventeen roll books, 1896-1913 with notations in some of them and a catalog of the school. Items contained in the Pickell Collection.

Lincoln Institute, Lincoln Ridge, Kentucky.
Files, 1909-1970. (KeSCF)

Incomplete files of annual reports with individual names included. Also known as the Lincoln School.

White, David Oliver. "Hartford's African Schools, 1830-1868." *Connecticut Historical Society Bulletin*, 39(1974) 47-53.

I. MISCELLANEOUS SOURCES

1. Clipping Files
2. Funeral Programs
3. Insurance Records
4. Marriage Ceremony Programs
5. Medical Records
6. Scrapbooks
7. Maps

Most public libraries--city, county, state, and national --maintain collections that include materials that do not fit neatly into specific categories of information and are relegated to a single or multiple collections. The miscellaneous materials may be found among manuscripts or estate papers, in clipping files, or in *genealogy rooms* or collections if so designated by the organizers of the collections. Miscellaneous sources include clipping files, funeral programs, insurance records, marriage ceremony programs, medical records, scrapbooks, and maps. Many of these materials are found in most homes and are often overlooked because they seem so obvious.

1. Clipping Files

Most public libraries maintain clipping files as do clubs and societies. Clippings may be located in vertical files and appear in scrapbooks as do photographs, programs, and memorabilia. Some agencies maintain recognized clipping files that include newspaper clippings of marriages, obituaries, and other events in people's lives. Notable clipping files include the Moorland-Spingarn collection at Howard University, the Schomburg Collection of the New York Public Library, and a number of historically black college and university libraries.

Indiana State Library,
Clipping File, ca. 1920- to date.

Includes clippings from Indiana newspapers, periodicals, and books and is arranged by name and subject. Although not designated by race, there are biographical and genealogical finds for Afro-Americans.

Schomburg Center for Research in Black Culture
New York, New York.
Schomburg Clipping File, 1926 - to date.

Contains nearly one million pages of materials documenting the black experience in America and includes newspapers, periodicals, broadsides, book reviews, menus, and other ephemera to record black activities and achievements.

2. Funeral Programs.

Programs of funeral services generally include a biographical sketch of the deceased including birth and death dates, parents, siblings, spouse, and offspring. Funeral directors, churches, clubs, and organizations to which the deceased belonged; agencies with which the individual was affiliated, and family members often keep funeral programs. Local, state, and special libraries and collections may keep programs of services of noted members in the community. Colleges and universities may keep copies of programs of funerals of deceased alumni in alumni files or in the school's archives.

3. Insurance Records.

Insurance records may include early insurance records of slave traders, slaveholders who insured slaves as property; individual health, life, and property insurance policies held by private citizens, and insurance coverage maintained by employers for their workers. Such southern-based insurance companies as the Fulton Insurance Company, the Merchants Insurance Company--both of Mobile, Alabama; Southern Mutual of Georgia, and Lynchburg Hose and Fire Company Insurance Company of North America insured slave-traders as did the Charter Oak Insurance Company of Hartford, Connecticut. Records of insurance (policies) of private individuals may be found in the personal effects of the insured and in collections of private papers in institutions and agencies. Insurance records are expected to include the name(s) of the insured, birth dates, beneficiaries, and relationship of the beneficiaries to the deceased.

4. Marriage Ceremony Programs.

Copies of programs of wedding ceremonies will be found in similar locations as other resources of private origin. Genealogical information of the marriage program include the names of the bride and groom, names of participants in the wedding, and often their relationships to the bride and groom, the city, state, and date of the occasion.

5. Medical Records.

Medical records may be public or private. Private medical records include physicians' and dentists' financial record books, patient records, and treatment records.

Medical records are available for some slaves as seen in records of physicians who attended plantations. Medical records of free men in the north and south appear among physicians' and dentists' private records and among hospital records where a patient was treated. Medical records of newly freed men who reported to federal hospitals such as the Engineer Hospital at Mobile, Alabama, and the Chimboraza General Hospital in Richmond, Virginia, are in the National Archives. Records of hospitals in large urban areas with significant Afro-American populations are good potential sources for medical record information. Historically black medical schools with out-patient clinics and hospitals are further sources. The health departments of local areas and state archives may have supervision of medical records of public agencies.

Many pre-integration all-black hospitals have closed in more recent years, but the records of these agencies are good sources of genealogical information.

Gifford, (Dr.) William Howell. Clay County, Indiana.
Records, 1851-66. (IndSL)

Records list patients by name with indication of race.

Hardison, Dr. Hardy. Albemarle Sound Area, North Carolina.
Record Book, 1849-66. (SoHCUNC)

Physician's account book indicates both black and white patients.

Mississippi (Counties) Adams, Hinds and Warren.
Medical Records, 1880-1940. (MsDAR)

Designation by race with some records restricted.

Physician's Record Book, Washington, North Carolina, 1855-1858. (SoHCUNC)

Physician's records list numerous individuals described as mulatto. No other racial or ethnic designations are noted.

6. Scrapbooks.

Daughters of the American Revolution, General Zollicoffer Chapter.
Papers, 1910-1960 (TeSL)

Scrapbook with newspaper story on the life of Guy Washington, a former slave who served in General Hood's command during the Civil War.

Mary P. Morris.
Scrapbooks, 1877-1923. (CnHS)

Social items and obituaries clipped from four area newspapers.

Tennessee State Library and Archives.
Scrapbook Collection, 1890-1937. 2 vols.

Scrapbooks concerning Nashville, Tennessee, including materials about Afro-Americans.

7. Maps.

Boley, Oklahoma.
Fire Insurance Maps, 1906, 1908. (OkHS)

Boley had a large black population and maps include specific names of individuals.

Wellston, Oklahoma.
Fire Insurance Maps, 1899, 1902, 1908. (OkHS)

Wellston was a town with a significant number of Afro-American residents.

PART III

PUBLIC RECORDS AND RESOURCES

A. FEDERAL RECORDS AND RESOURCES
  1. Freedmen's Bureau
  2. Federal Census Records--Population and Mortality Schedules
     General References
  3. Other Federal Records in the National Archives
     a. Bureau of Customs
     b. Department of the Treasury
     c. Adjutant General's Office
     d. Department of the Interior
  4. Military Records and Resources
     a. General References
     b. Wars
        (1) War of 1775-1783 (Revolutionary War)
            References
        (2) War of 1812-1814 (British-American War)
        (3) War of 1846-1848 (Mexican War)
        (4) Wars of 1854-1891 (Indian Wars)
        (5) War of 1861-1865 (Civil War)
        (6) War of 1898 (Spanish-American War)
     c. Military Pensions
     d. Military Cemeteries
     e. Confederate Military Records
  5. Federal Courts
  6. Penal Institutions
  7. Miscellaneous Records

Public records are a major source of genealogical information. Public records, for the purpose of this work, are those that emanate largely from an agency of federal, state, or local government. Other resources, such as city and telephone directories that are inclusive and not confined to a selected segment of the population and are published for the purpose of public use, are also included in this section.

Federal records evolve from an agency of the federal government and include military records, veteran's pensions, and bounty land grants, census of population, mortality statistics, and freedmen's records. Courts, prisons, hospitals, schools, and other agencies and institutions that are units of federal government are included.

State and local governments are directly concerned with the daily lives of the American people, thereby creating many useful records. Records of the cities, counties, and states include vital records of births, marriages, deaths, and land transactions. Units of government supervise elections; agencies of welfare care for the sick and indigent, the aged and orphans, and the mentally impaired. They establish schools, regulate health and safety, supervise prisons and other types of institutions. Local governments collect taxes, and local courts handle civil and criminal cases.

The social and legal statutes prior to 1865, as has been stated elsewhere, excluded nearly all but free blacks from most public records. Slaves may be named in land records since they were treated as chattel or property. They appear in special schedules of census largely as numerical listings, and some few are listed by name. Separate registers of both slaves and black free men were issued by various states in both the north and south. Tax records of slave holders often include the names of slaves. Early court records include permits and licenses to conduct slave trading, probate records that list slaves by name, trials of slaves and black free men, and marriage and cohabitation bonds. Later public records (since 1865) should include Afro-Americans as other citizens. Many of the later records designate the race of subject.

A. FEDERAL RECORDS AND RESOURCES

1. Freedmen's Bureau.

The Bureau of Refugees, Freedmen, and Abandoned Lands was established in the War Department on March 3, 1865, to issue supplies to the destitute men and women recently emancipated, take charge of abandoned lands to lease and ultimately sell, and have control of all subjects related to refugees and freedmen. The Bureau ended its main work in 1869; its educational work continued until 1872.

Records in the Bureau's collection are now on microfilm and housed in the National Archives. They include marriage contracts, school reports, records of the depositors of the Savings and Trust Company, and correspondence on the operations of the Bureau.

Perhaps the more distinctive holdings in the Bureau's collection are the *records of the Office of the Comptroller* that include the *register of signatures of depositions in branches of Freedmen's Savings and Trust Company from 1865-*

1874. Twenty-seven rolls of microfilm list information for each deposition including account number, name of depositor, date, place of birth, place reared, resident, age, complexion, name of employer or occupation, spouse, children, parents, siblings, signatures, and for some the names of former owners and plantations. The collection is arranged by account number rather than by name. However, records are grouped by states and city branches.

Groups of Freedmen's Bureau Records in the National Archives include:

Record Group 101. Records of the office of the Controller of the Currency
Register of Signatures of Depositors in Branches of Freedmen's Savings and Trust Company from 1865-1874.

Information on each depositor includes: name, date, account number, place of birth, where reared, residence, age, complexion, name of employee, occupation, spouse, children, parents, and siblings.

Record Group 101. Alabama.
Alabama branches with deposits for Huntsville and Mobile.

Record Group 101. Arkansas.
Arkansas branch with deposits for Little Rock.

Record Group 101. District of Columbia.
City with deposits recorded for Washington.

Record Group 101. Florida.
Branch at Tallahassee with deposits recorded.

Record Group 101. Georgia.

Record Group 101. Kentucky.
Kentucky branches with deposits recorded for Lexington and Louisville.

Record Group 101. Louisiana.

Record Group 101. Maryland.
Record of deposits for Baltimore.

Record Group 101. Mississippi.
Mississippi branches with records of deposits in Columbia, Natchez, and Vicksburg.

Record Group 101. Missouri.
Missouri branches with deposits recorded for St. Louis.

Record Group 101. New York.
New York branches with deposits recorded for New York City.

Record Group 101. Pennsylvania.
Pennsylvania branches with deposits recorded for Philadelphia.

Record Group 101. South Carolina.
South Carolina branches with deposits recorded for Beaufort and Charleston.

Record Group 101. Tennessee.
Tennessee branches with deposits recorded for Memphis and Nashville.

Record Group 101. Virginia.
Virginia branches with recorded deposits for Lynchburg, Norfolk, and Richmond.

Record Group 105. *Records of the Bureau of Refugees, Freedmen, and Abandoned Lands*

A second group of Freedmen's Bureau records are the volumes of correspondence sent and received dealing with the operations of the Bureau. The Education Division of this group includes monthly reports of pupil progress, roster of teachers and secretaries. School reports of the Assistant Commissioner and/or Superintendent of Education and the Field Offices of the various states are included.

Record Group 105. Alabama.

Alabama records contain Education Division Reports; letters sent and received; narratives of conditions and rosters of personnel.

Record Group 105. Arkansas.

Arkansas records contain school reports.

Record Group 105. District of Columbia.

District of Columbia group contains school reports.

Record Group 105. Florida.

Contains records of schools in Florida.

Record Group 105. Georgia.

Record Group 105. Kentucky.

Contains school records.

Record Group 105. Mississippi.

This group contains school reports, correspondence sent and received; station books and rosters; labor contracts between planters and freedmen; register of indentured servants and marriages, August 1865-May 1866. Name and age of orphans, color and age of married couples, and minister and witnesses.

Record Group 105. Missouri.
School records for Missouri.

Record Group 105. North Carolina.

Record Group 105. Tennessee.

Records contain school reports, letters sent and received, leases, indentures, labor contracts and registers of plantations.

Record Group 105. Texas.

Contains Texas school reports.

Record Group 105. Virginia.

Records contain school reports for Virginia.

2. Federal Census Records--Population and Mortality Schedules.

The first dicennial census of the United States was in 1790. The first twelve censuses of the United States, 1790-1900, were conducted without benefit of a permanent office. Supervisors of the first nine censuses, 1790-1870, were marshals of the United States judicial districts. The Bureau of the Census was established as a permanent office by act of Congress on March 6, 1902. The major functions of the Bureau are authorized by the Constitution, which provides that a census of population shall be taken every ten years. Information collected is strictly confidential and is used for statistical purposes only. The principal functions of the Bureau include the dicennial census of population and housing, quinquential census of agriculture, and state and local governments. The Bureau conducts special censuses at the request and expense of state and local governments. Upon request the Bureau makes searches of dicennial census records and furnishes certificates to individuals for use as evidence of age, relationship, or place of birth. A fee is charged for this service.

The census schedules from 1800 are in the National Archives in Washington, D.C., and are available for personal searching.

The 1850 census was the first to enumerate every free person in individual households. Designers of this census considered that vital information as birth, marriage, and death could be collected through the census medium. Thus began the mortality schedules. In compliance with an act of Congress, a separate schedule was devised for the purpose of collecting data about persons who had died during the census year. Mortality schedules exist for the years 1850, 1860, 1870, 1880, and the limited census of 1885. In 1918 and 1919 mortality schedules for the census years 1850-1880 were removed from federal custody, and each state was allowed to secure those relating to itself. Those not claimed by the states were given to the National Society of the Daughters of the American Revolution and placed in the Society's Library. The DAR holds the original schedules for Arizona, Colorado, Georgia, Kentucky, Louisiana, Tennessee, and the District of Columbia. Less than 8 percent of the population that died in the years 1850-1885 may be included in the mortality schedules.

General References

Brewer, Mary Marie. *Index to Census Schedules in Printed Form.* Huntsville, Ark: Century Enterprises, 1969.

Census of Pensioners, a General Index for Revolutionary or Military Service (1840), prepared by the Genealogical Society of the Church of Jesus Christ Latter-Day Saints. Baltimore: Genealogical Publishing Co., 1965.

Franklin, Neil W. "Availability of Federal Population Census Schedules in the States." *National Genealogical Society Quarterly*, 50(1962): 19.

United States. Department of Commerce. "Your Name Is Somewhere in the Census Records." (Form BC-628) Pittsburg, Kan.: Bureau of the Census, 1976.

Federal Population Schedules

1790- First Census of the United States. The population of the country was divided into number of free white males in a family under 16 and over, white females without an age breakdown, and other free persons including blacks. The census is arranged by state and county.

1800- Second census of the United States. Same as the 1790.

1810- Third Census of the United States. Same as 1790.

1820- Fourth Census of the United States. Lists free blacks who were heads of households by name. Slaves and free blacks in white households are not named but numbered within age groups (under 14; 14-26; 26-45; and 45 and over). Data on persons engaged in agriculture, commerce, and manufacturing are recorded. Free black farmers are mentioned briefly in this census.

1830- Fifth Census of the United States. Same as 1820 except age grouping differs: under 10; 10-25; 25-36; 36-55; 55-100; and 100 and over. Agriculture, manufacturing, and commerce data are not included in this census.

1840- Sixth Census of the United States. Same as the Fifth except this census includes an enumeration of Revolutionary War pensioners of the federal government.

1850- Seventh Census of the United States. The first census to list by name every free inhabitant of a household and indicate age, sex, color (black, mulatto and sometimes "Indian"), place of birth, profession, trade or occupation for males over fifteen, and other personal facts. This census is divided into free and slave schedules and arranged by state and county. Slave schedules list number of slaves by age and sex under owner's name, and occasionally slave names are included. Free black farmers are included in a special census for this year including the name of the farmer and a description of the land, animals, and equipment. The 1850 census has recently been computerized by the LDS library in Salt Lake City, Utah, and is available through the LDS branches in book form and indexed by name. A separate schedule begun with this census for persons who died in the census year is called the "mortality" schedule.

1860- Eighth Census of the United States. Varies from 1850 in that females over fifteen have their profession, trade, or occupation listed and slaves over one hundred years of age are named and place of birth stated. There is also information on the number of slaves freed by each owner. A mortality census was also taken for the year.

1870- Ninth Census of the United States. This is the first federal census which includes the names of *all* people counted. This census is particularly significant as it is the first schedule taken since the Emancipation Proclamation. There is a slave schedule in this census. The symbols "Y" for Chinese and "I" for Indian are included in the color designations.

1880- Tenth Census of the United States. This census was the first to give the relationship of a family member to the head of the household as well as the birthplace of each person and of the parents of each person listed. This census has a Soundex for all families with children under age ten. The Soundex system is a method of indexing by the sound of the last name. This census is arranged by state and county.

1890- Eleventh Census of the United States. This census was almost completely destroyed in 1921 by a fire in the basement of the Commerce Department Building. An index at the National Archives lists the names of householders in the few surviving schedules. This index is available on microfilm (2 rolls) and relates to schedules arranged by state for Alabama, the District of Columbia, Georgia, Illinois, Minnesota, New Jersey, New York, North Carolina, Ohio, South Dakota, and Texas. The schedules are also on microfilm.

1900- Twelfth Census of the United States. Same as the 1880 with the addition of socioeconomic facts for each family. There is a Soundex for the 1900 census which includes all people, not just those who lived in households.

Special Enumerations Taken
by the Federal Government

1857 - Minnesota Territory

1864 - Arizona Territory (Originals are with the Secretary of State in Phoenix)

1866 - Arizona Territory (Certain counties)

1867 - Arizona Territory (Certain counties)

1869 - Arizona Territory (Certain counties)

1880 - Special census of Indians not taxed

1885 - Colorado, Dakota Territory, Florida, Nebraska, and New Mexico Territory. This census was taken by states and territories on a federal option and promise of partial reimbursement. Similar in form to the 1880 census, this special census is relevant to the Afro-American farmer.

1907 - Oklahoma (Seminole County)

Population and Mortality
Schedules by State

Alabama.
Population Schedules, 1820-80 and 1900 (NAr)
1830-1880 (AlAr) and public libraries; 1860
Slave Schedules (AlAr)
Mortality Schedules, 1850-1880 (AlAr)

Alaska.
Population Schedules, 1870-1880 and 1900 (NAr)

Arizona.
Population Schedules, 1870-1880 and 1900 (NAr);
1870-1880 (AzML)
Territorial Censuses, 1864, 1866, 1867, 1869
(NAr); (AzHS)
Mortality Schedules, 1870, 1880 (NAr)

Arkansas.
Population Schedules, 1830-1880 and 1900 (NAr); 1830-1880 (ArHS)
Mortality Schedules, 1850-1880 (ArHS)

California.
Population Schedules, 1850-1880 and 1900 (NAr); 1850-1880 (Colleges and public libraries in the state.)
Mortality Schedules, 1850-1880 (CaSL)

Colorado.
Population Schedules, 1860-1880, 1885, and 1900 (NAr);
1860-1880 (DCoPL); 1860-1880 and 1885 (CoU)
Mortality Schedules, 1870-1880 and 1885 (NAr); 1870-1880 (DAR)

Connecticut.
Population Schedules, 1790-1880 and 1900 (NAr);
Mortality Schedules, 1850-1880 (CnSL, GLLDS)

Delaware.
Population Schedules, 1790-1880 and 1900 (NAr, DelHS)
Mortality Schedules, 1850-1880 (DelPAr)

District of Columbia.
Population Schedules, 1800-1880 and 1900 (NAr); 1800-1880 (DAR)

Florida.
Population Schedules, 1830-1880 (NAr, FiSU); 1900 and Territorial Census (NAr) and other schedules at other libraries in the state. Mortality Schedules, 1885 (NAr)

Georgia.
Population Schedules, 1820 (GaAr); 1820-1900 (NAr); 1830, 1850, 1880 (GaU)
Mortality Schedules, 1850, 1860, 1870, and 1880 (NAr, DAR)
Schedule of Slave Owners, 1850-1860 (includes all Georgia counties)
Owsley Charts. A collection of data on land and slave information taken from all counties in the state in the Federal Census of Georgia, 1840-1860.

Idaho.
Population Schedules, 1870-1880 and 1900 (NAr); 1870-1880 (IdHS)
Mortality Schedules, 1870-1880 (IdHS)

Illinois.
Population Schedules, 1810-1880 and 1900. 1818 Territorial Census (NAr). Other records in various public and college libraries in the State.
Mortality Schedules, 1850-1990 (NAr, IlSAr)

Indiana.
Population Schedules, 1820-1880 and 1900 (NAr); 1820-1880 (ALPLI) and other libraries in the state.
Mortality Schedules, 1850-1880 (IndSL)

Iowa.
Population Schedules, 1840-1880, 1900, 1844-1846. Territorial Census (NAr); 1840-1880 (NIaU)
Mortality Schedules, 1850-1880 (IaHS)

Kansas.
Population Schedules, 1860-1880 (NAr, KaSHS, Wichita and Lawrence Public Libraries); 1900 (NAr)
Mortality Schedules, 1860-1880 (NAr, DAR, KaSHS)

Kentucky.
Population Schedules, 1810-1880 (NAr, FilCK, KeHS); 1900 (NAr). Also public libraries.
Mortality Schedules, 1850-1880 (NAr, DAR)
Special Census, 1890 (NAr, FilCK, KeHS)

Louisiana.
Population Schedules, 1810-1880 (NAr, LSU); 1900 (NAr)
Mortality Schedules, 1850-1880 (NAr, DAR)
Special Census, 1890 (NAr, LSU)

Maine.
Population Schedules, 1790-1880 and 1900 (NAr); 1790-1860 (MeHS)
Mortality Schedules, 1850-1880 (MeVS); 1850-1870 (GLLDS)
Special Census, 1890 (NAr)

Maryland.
Population Schedules, 1790-1900 (NAr);

1800-1890 (MdSCPA). Other libraries in the state have some schedules.
Mortality Schedules, 1850-1880 (MdSCPA)
Special Census, 1890 (NAr, MdHS)

Massachusetts.
Population Schedules, 1790-1880 and 1900 (NAr); 1790-1880 (MaUA)
Mortality Schedules, 1850-1880 (NAr, DAR, MaSAr)
Special Census, 1890 (NAr)

Michigan.
Population Schedules, 1820-1880 and 1900 (NAr); 1820-1880 (MiU, BrHLDPL, CMiUMP)
Mortality Schedules, 1860-1880 (NAr, MiHS)
Special Census, 1890 (NAr, MiSL, CMiUMP)

Minnesota.
Population Schedules, 1850-1880 and 1900; 1849 and 1857 Territorial Census (NAr); 1850-1880 (MnHS, MnSAr)
Mortality Schedules, 1850-1870 (DAR); 1870 (NAr)
Special Census, 1890 (NAr and GACStP)

Mississippi.
Population Schedules, 1830-1880 (NAr, MsSAr, MSU); and 1900 (NAr). And at Aberdeen, Boonesville, Cleveland, Greenwood, and Hattiesburg Libraries. Meridan has 1830-1880 population schedules on microfilm. Territorial Census for 1805, 1810, and 1816 (MsSAr) Mortality Schedules, 1850-1880 (MsSAr) Special Census, 1890 (NAr, MsSAr, MsUHa)

Montana.
Population Schedules, 1860-1880 and 1900 (NAr)
Mortality Schedules, 1870-1880 (NAr, MtHS)
Special Census, 1890 (NAr)
Mortality Schedules, 1850-1880 (MtHS)
Special Census, 1890 (NAr)

Missouri.
Population Schedules, 1830-1880 and 1900 (NAr); 1830-1880 (MoHS, MoSLPL)
Mortality Schedules, 1850-1880 (MoSHS)
Special Census, 1890 (NAr, StPL, MoHS)

Nebraska.
Population Schedules, 1860-1880, 1885 (NAr);

1860-1880 (NbSHS)
Mortality Schedules, 1860-1880, 1885 (NAr);
1860-1880 (NvU and other libraries in the state)
Mortality Schedules, 1860-1880 (NvSHS); 1870 (DAR)

New Hampshire.
Population Schedules, 1790-1880 and 1900 (NAr);
1790 and 1880 (NHSL)
Mortality Schedules, 1850-1880 (NHSL); 1850-1870
(GLLDS)
Special Census, 1890 (NAr, NHSL)

New Jersey.
Population Schedules, 1830-1880 (NAr, NJSL and
public libraries and historical societies in the
state have some schedules)
Mortality Schedules, 1850-1880 (DAr, NJSL)
Special Census, 1890 (NAr, NJBArH)

New Mexico.
Population Schedules, 1850-1880, 1885, and 1900
(NAr); 1850 and 1880 (NMU)
Mortality Schedules, 1885 (Nr, NMU)
Special Census, 1890 (NAr, NMU)

New York.
Population Schedules, 1790-1880 and 1900 (NAr):
1800-1860 (NYGBS); 1800-1880 NYScC). Also
available in libraries of colleges and cities in
the state.
Mortality Schedules, 1850-1880 (NYSL)
Special Census, 1890 (NAr, NYPL) and some other
libraries in the state.

North Carolina.
Population Schedules, 1790-1900 (NAr, NCAr)
Libraries throughout the state have some schedules
for some years.
Mortality Schedules, 1850-1880 (NAr, NCAr)
Special Census, 1890 (NAr, NCU). Some public
libraries in the state have schedules.

North Dakota.
Population Schedules, 1880-1885 (NDSHS)
Mortality Schedules, 1880 (GLLDS); 1885 (NDSHS)

Ohio.
Population Schedules, 1820-1880 and 1900 (NAr);

1820-1880 (OhSHS) and other public and college libraries in the state.
Mortality Schedules, 1850-1860 and 1880 (NAr)
Special Census, 1890 (NAr, OhU)

Oklahoma.
Population Schedules, 1860 and 1890 Territorial (NAr, OkHS); 1900 (NAr)
Mortality--None
Special Census, 1890 (NAr)

Oregon.
Population Schedules, 1850-1880 (NAr, OrSAr, OrHS) 1900 (NAr)
Mortality Schedules, 1850-1880 (OrSAr)
Special Census, 1890 (NAr, OrSAr, OrHS)

Pennsylvania.
Population Schedules, 1790-1880 and 1900 (NAr); 1800-1880 (PeSL, PiU) and some other libraries in the state have some schedules for some years.
Mortality Schedules, 1850-1880 (PeSL)
Special Census, 1890 (NAr, PiU) and a few other libraries in the state.

Rhode Island.
Population Schedules, 1790-1880 and 1900 (NAr); 1800-1880 (RISL, PrC)
Special Census, 1890 (NAr)

South Carolina.
Population Schedules, 1790-1880 and 1900 (NAr); 1800-1880 (SCSAr) and libraries of counties, colleges and historical societies have schedules for some years.
Mortality Schedules, 1850-1880 (NAr, DAR, SCSAr)
Special Census, 1890 (NAr, SCSAr, WinC)

South Dakota.
Population Schedules, 1860-1880 and 1885 (NAr, SDSHS)
Mortality Schedules, 1885 (SDSHS)
Special Census, 1890 (NAr, SDSHS)

Tennessee.
Population Schedules, 1820-1880 and 1900 (NAr) 1820-1880 (TeSL) Fayetteville, Chattanooga, and Memphis public libraries.

Mortality Schedules, 1850-1880 (NAr, DAR)
Special census, 1890 (NAr, TeSL, EaTU)

Utah.
Population Schedules, 1850-1880 and 1900 (NAr); 1850-1880 (GLLDS, BriYU)

Vermont.
Population Schedules, 1790-1880 and 1900 (NAr) 1790-1880 (VtU)
Mortality Schedules, 1850-1880 (VtSL); 1850-1860 (DAR); 1870 (NAr, TxSL)
Special Census, 1890 (NAr)

Virginia.
Population Schedules, 1810-1880 and 1900 (NAr); 1810-1880 (ViSL, ViU)
Mortality Schedules, 1860-1870; 1860 (NAr, DuU, GLLDS)
Special Census, 1890 (NAr, ViU) and several public libraries in the state.

Washington (State).
Population Schedules, 1860-1880 (NAr, WaSL, SpPl, WaSHS); 1900 (NAr)
Mortality Schedules, 1860-1880 (DAR, WaSL)
Special Census, 1890 (NAr, WaSL, WaSHS, SpPL)

West Virginia.
Population Schedules, 1870-1880 and 1900 (NAr); 1870-1880 WVAr) and several libraries in the state have population schedules.
Mortality Schedules, 1860-1880 (WVAr)
Special Census, 1890 (NAr) and in a number of public libraries in the state.

Wisconsin.
Population Schedules, 1820-1880 and 1900 (NAr); 1820-1880 (WiSHS): 1830-1880 (MilPL); Territorial Census for 1836, 1842, 1846, 1847 (NAr) Mortality Schedules, 1850-1880 (WiSHS); 1850-1870 (DAR); 1860-1870 (MilPL) Special Census, 1890 (NAr, MilPL, WiU)

Wyoming.
Population Schedules, 1860-1880 and 1900 (NAr); 1860-1880 (WyAr)
Mortality Schedules, 1870-1880 (DAR)
Special Census, 1890 (NAr, WyAr)

3. Other Federal Records in the National Archives.
   a. Bureau of Customs.
      Record Group 36, Records of the Bureau of Customs (NAr)

      Time book for mechanics and slaves employed at Fort Morgan, Arkansas, 1861-1862.

      Record Group 36, Records of the Bureau of Customs. (NAr)

      Records contain manifests for New Orleans, 1819-1856.

      Record Group 36, Records of the Bureau of Customs. (NAr)

      Slave manifests for Savannah, Georgia, before 1808.

      Record Group 36, U.S. Customs Service. (NAr) Slave Manifest, 1789-1808.

      Masters of ships bringing cargo into the United States from abroad had to submit a manifest or list of all goods aboard. Manifest of human cargo required a name, sex, age, and height of each individual.

   b. Department of the Treasury
      Record Group 56, General Records of the Department of the Treasury. (NAr)

      Third Special Agency. Supervisory Special Agent's dealing with freedmen before the Freedmen's Bureau was established.

      Record Group 56, General Records of the Department of the Treasury. (NAr)

      Third Special Agency. Supervisory Special Agent's dealing with freedmen, 1863-1865, before the establishment of the Freedmen's Bureau. (Ark)

      Record Group 56, General Records of the Department of the Treasury. (NAr)

      Third Special Agency: Dealings with Freedmen before the Freedmen's Bureau was established. (Fla)

Record Group 56, General Records of the Department of the Treasury. (NAr)

Third Special Agency: Supervisory Special Agent's dealing with Freedmen before the Freedmen's Bureau was established, 1863-1865. (La)

Record Group 56, General Records of the Department of the Treasury (NAr)

Third Special Agency: Supervisory Special Agent's dealing with freedmen before the Freedmen's Bureau was established. (Miss)

Record Group 56, General Records of the Department of the Treasury. (NAr)

Contains records of Third Special Agency including 1863-1865 dealings in regard to freedmen before the establishment of the Freedmen's Bureau. (Tex)

Record Group 56, General Records of the Department of Treasury. (NAr)

Fifth Special Agency: Port Royal
Correspondence records of the Sea Islands, South Carolina with reports of the earliest care and education of freedmen.

c. Adjutant General's Office
Record Group 94, Records of the Adjutant General's Office, 1780-1817 (NAr)

Register of claims by the Slave Claims Commission for Kentucky, 1864-1867

Record Group 94, Records of the Adjutant General's Office, 1780-1817. (NAr)

Slave Claims Commission's register for Maryland, 1864-67.

Record Group 94, Records of the Adjutant General's Office, 1780-1817. (NAr)

Slave Claims Commission, Register of claims for West Virginia, 1864-1867.

d. Department of the Interior
Record Group 48, Records of the Office of the Secretary of the interior. (NAr)

Contains the record appointments, 1849-1908, and lists of personnel at the Freedmen's Hospital at Howard University. Includes all registers of deeds in the District of Columbia, as well as biographical material on prominent blacks.

Secretary of the Interior

Final Rolls of Citizens and Freedmen of the Five Civilized Tribes of the Indian Territory (NAr and Federal Records Center at Kansas)

4. Military Records.

There are two basic kinds of military records: records of service of military men and records of veterans benefits. The National Archives is the major source for records of persons who served in the several wars in which the United States was involved. The War Department Archives and the Library of Congress also have records. Records of military service after 1914 are in the National Personnel and Records Center in St. Louis, Missouri. Other early records may be found in state and local depositories and in collections of genealogical and historical societies and organizations.

The National Archives has issued several helpful publications with specific reference to location and use of military resources. Some states have developed lists of military records available in the state archives. Several authors have written books on the roles of black servicemen in specific wars and in specific military ranks. These sources have served to make the public more aware of the long history of blacks in the defense of the nation, having served in one role or another in every war since and including the Revolutionary War. These sources include names, dates, and contributions of individual personalities.

a. General References.

The Black Military Experience in the American West. New York: Liveright, 1971.

Fletcher, Marvin. *The Black Soldier and Officer in the United States Army, 1891-1917.* Columbia, Mo.: University of Missouri Press, 1974.

Fowler, Arlen L. *The Black Infantry in the West, 1869-1891*. Westport, Conn.: Greenwood Press, 1971.

Following the Civil War Afro-Americans served in the regular Army. This work covers the subject.

Johnson, Jesse J., editor. *Black Armed Forces Officers, 1731-1971*. A Documented Pictoral History. Hampton, Va.: 1971.

Leckie, William H. *The Buffalo Soldiers: A Narrative of the Negro Cavalry in the West*. Norman, Okla.: University of Oklahoma Press, 1967.

The Medical and Surgical History of the War of Rebellion. 6 vols. Washington, D.C.: GPO, 1888.

Includes some names of black patients, their ailments, the hospital, and the regiment.

Tabular Analysis of the Records of the U.S. Colored Troops and Their Predecessor Units in the National Archives of the United States, compiled by Joseph B. Ross. Washington, D.C.: United States Adjutant General's Office, 1973. (NAr)

b. Wars
(1) War of 1775-1783 (Revolutionary War)
References:

Greene, Robert Ewell. *Black Courage, 1775-1783. Documentation of Black Participation in the American Revolution*. Washington, D.C.: Daughters of the American Revolution, 1984.

This is a study of Revolutionary War pension records of 5,000 black men who served in that war. Depicts subject's social background and includes biographical sketches.

Jackson, Luther Porter, "Virginia Negro Soldiers and Seamen in the American Revolution." *Journal of Negro History*. 27(1942): 247-87.

Includes a list of black Virginia servicemen who fought in the war.

Moore, George H. *Historical Notes on the Employment of Negroes in the American Army of the Revolution.* New York: 1862. (CtHS)

Nell, William Cooper. *The Colored Patriots of the American Revolution.* New York: Arno Press, 1968.

Newman, Debra L. *Lists of Black Servicemen Compiled from the War Department Collection of Revolutionary War Records.* Special List 36. Washington, D.C.: National Archives and Records Service, 1974.

Quarles, Benjamin. *The Negro in the American Revolution.* Chapel Hill, N.C.: University of North Carolina Press, 1961.

White, David Oliver. *Connecticut's Black Soldiers, 1775-1783.* Chester, Pa.: Pequoh Press, 1973. (Connecticut Bicentennial Series, No. 4)

(2) War of 1812-1814 (British-American War)

It is generally understood that army regulations specifically excluded blacks from activities in the War of 1812 in roles other than as cooks, stewards, and servants.

(3) War of 1846-1848 (Mexican War)

Records of this period include:

Johnson, Thomas S.
Papers, 1839-1869. (WiHS)

Papers cover the 127th Regiment of U.S. Colored Troops (Pennsylvania)

(4) Wars of 1854-1891 (Indian Wars)

Texas Historical Society. Circle M. Collection.

DeGalyer Foundation. Library Collection, Dallas. Fort Davis National Historic Site, El Paso. Have military records of "buffalo soldiers," 1854-91 and other black troops who served in the Indian Wars.

Indian War Papers, 1850-1880 (CaAr)

Includes primarily muster rolls, correspond-dences, loyalty oaths, and receipts.

(5) War of 1861-1865 (Civil War)

Bates, Samuel P. *History of Pennsylvania Volunteers, 1861-1865.* 5 vols. Harrisburg, Pa.: B. Singerly, 1869-1971.

Includes designation of black volunteers in specific infantries.

Brewer, James H. *The Confederate Negro.* Durham, N.C.: Duke University Press, 1969.

An information source on blacks who worked for the Confederacy during the Civil War.

Chenery, William H. *The Fourteenth Regiment, Rhode Island Heavy Artillery (Colored) in the War to Preserve the Union, 1861-1865.* Providence, RI: Snow and Tarnham, 1898.

Rosters of servicemen in specific units noted.

Civil War Collection, 1866-1867. California State Archives.

Civil War and Military Collection, 1851-1869. California State Library.

Contains letters and diaries of several members of Colored Troops regiments.

Clark, Peter H. *The Black Brigade of Cincinnati.* New York: Arno Press, 1969.

Cornish, Dudley Taylor. *Kansas Negro Regiments in the Civil War.* Topeka, Ka.: State of Kansas Commission on Civil Rights, 1969.

Griffith, David J., MD. 1862-1864. Papers, 1862-1864 (IlHS)

Civil War medical records reporting the care of black troops and the employment of black workers.

Griffin, John A.
Papers, 1860-1869 (IlHS)

Diary written in 1862-1863 when Griffin was a private in Company D, 17th Illinois Infantry. Letters of soldiers in the 53rd U.S. Colored Troops.

Hooker, Joseph. *Military Papers, 1861-1864.*
Military Papers, 1861-1864 (HLSMCa)

Papers include information on freed slaves.

Iowa. Adjutant General's Office. *Roster of Iowa Soldiers in the War of the Rebellion. 32nd-48th Regiments Infantry, 1st Regiment African Infantry and 1st-4th Batteries Light Artillery.* Vol. 5, Des Moines: E.H. Engist, State Printer, 1908-1911. (IaHS)

Names of members of Iowa's only black regiment during Civil War are detailed in this source.

Marcus, Roland. *Service Records of Stanford Connecticut Black Soldiers during the Civil War.* Stanford: Stanford Historical Society, 1972.

Mickley, Jeremiah Marion. *The Forty-Third Regiment United States Colored Troops.* Gettysburg, Pa.: J.E.Wible, 1866.

Military Records Collection, 1861-1875. (TeSL)

Collection contains nearly a hundred reels of microfilm that includes an index to service records of black Union veterans from Tennessee.

Murden, Kenneth W., and Henry Putney Beers. *Guide to Federal Archives Relating to the Civil War.* Washington, D.C.: The National Archives, 1962.

Records of the Office of the Quarter Master General. Record Group 92, National Archives.

Records of the Provost Marshall General's Bureau, Record Group 110, National Archives.

National draft enrollments lists giving residence, age, race, profession, marital status and place of birth, 1863-1865 and emancipation applications, 1862-1863. Contains records of Civil War period including lists of black troops buried and ex-slaves who were contraband.

Strong, George W.
Papers, 1863-1908 (IaU)

Former Commander of Company H, 1st Regiment of Tennessee Infantry, African Descent and 5th Colored Infantry, Regiment 16th Corps, 1863-1865. Strong's papers include letters, memos, orders, and supply records of his command.

Wesley, Charles H. *Negro Americans in the Civil War*. Washington, D.C.: Association for the study of Negro Life and History, 1968.

———. *Ohio Negroes in the Civil War*. Publication of the Ohio Civil War Centennial Commission, No. 6. Columbus: Ohio Historical Society, 1962.

Whitney, Henry
Papers. (RtSU)

Civil War journal including information on blacks from West Virginia and information on students and applicants for command of colored troops.

Willis, George H.
Papers, 1836-1866. (BoU)

Collection of papers contains orders and supply records for the 118th Colored Infantry Regiment.

(6) War of 1898 (Spanish American War)
Shaffer, William Rufus
Papers, 1863-1904 (CaSL)

This collection includes letters and broadsides about Spanish-American War activities in Cuba collected by the Commander of the 17th U.S. Colored Infantry.

Cohabitation Records, 1866-1868.

Prior to 1865, slaves in North Carolina were not legally permitted to marry, although many of them lived together as husband and wife. Following the end of the Civil War, the North Carolina General Assembly enacted legislation on March 10, 1866, which ordered former slaves to have their marriages recorded. Originally, the marriage was to be registered before September 1, 1866, but in 1867 the deadline was extended to January 1, 1868. A twenty-five cent fee was paid in order for the marriage to be recorded.

Approximately 20,000 records of cohabitation have survived from thirty-nine counties. The number ranges from three records in Mitchell County to about 1,900 in Craven County. They show the name of the male, the name of the female, and the length of time they had lived together as husband and wife prior to 1866. The record also indicates before whom the statement was made. Cohabitation records usually are not indexed and many of them were entered in random order in record books. In a few counties, however, they were filed on individual forms which are arranged alphabetically by name of male.

Cohabitation records have survived from the following counties: Alexander, Alleghany, *Beaufort, Bertie, *Camden, *Catawba, *Craven, Currituck, Davidson, *Duplin, Edgecombe, *Forsyth, Franklin, Gates, *Granville, Halifax, Hyde, Iredell, Johnston, Lincoln, Mitchell, Nash, New Hanover, Orange, *Pasquotank, *Perquimans, Person, Pitt, Richmond, *Robeson, Stokes, Surry, Union, Wake, *Warren, Washington, Wayne, Wilkes, Wilson. Records of counties marked with an asterisk (*) are on microfilm, the originals remaining in the county.

STATE OF NORTH CAROLINA.

EDGECOMBE COUNTY.

ON this the 29 day of July 1866, personally appeared before me, W. W. Parker a Justice of the Peace in and for said County, Lewis Phillips and Sarah Ricks residents of said County, both of whom were lately slaves, but now emancipated, and acknowledge that they have cohabited as man and wife for 37 years.

4 Children

W. W. Parker J.P.

Cohabitation Record from Edgecombe County

Spanish American War, 1898-1900 (CaAr)

Includes primarily muster rolls, correspondences, loyalty oaths, and receipts.

Steward, Theophilus Gould. *The Colored Regulars in the United States Army, 1904.* Reprint American Negro History and Literature Series, No. 2, New York: Arno Press, 1969.

Covers the service of blacks in the Spanish American War.

c. Military Pensions

The Continental Congress passed the first pension act in 1776. Records exist for persons who have applied for pension benefits including former soldiers and their widows. These records are housed in the National Archives and are divided into seven major series: (1) Revolutionary War invalid series, (2) Revolutionary War service series, (3) "Old Wars" series, (4) War of 1812 series, (5) Mexican War Series, (6) Civil War and later series, and (7) Indian War series. Pension records in each series, except the Mexican, Civil and Indian Wars and later, are arranged alphabetically by the name of the veteran. The Pension Bureau at Washington, D.C., and the Pension Department of the Veterans Administration also maintains pension records.

Black soldiers were also involved in the Confederate Army. Confederate records are available in the National Archives, but the records are not considered as good as those for the Union soldiers. Individual southern states maintain records of pensioners who served in the Confederate Army. The states include Alabama, Arkansas, Florida, Georgia, Louisiana, Mississippi, North Carolina, South Carolina, Tennessee, Texas, and Virginia. These records are generally maintained by the state library or archives, and many collections are not as well organized as those at the National Archives. Resources include:

Census of Pensioners, a General Index for Revolutionary or Military Service (1840), prepared by the Genealogical Society of the Church of Jesus Christ Latter-Day Saints. Baltimore: Genealogical Publishing Co., 1965. (Addendum to the 1840 Census)

"Military Personnel Records in the North Carolina State Archives, 1918-1964." *North Carolina Archives Information Circular*, Number 11.

Tennessee Confederate Pension Applications, 1891. (TeSL)

Personal and family history included for both black and white veterans.

United States. Pension Bureau. *List of Pensioners on the Roll January 1, 1883*. 5 vols. Senate Executive Document 84, 4th Congress, 2nd Session, 1883. Reprint. Baltimore: Genealogical Publishing Co., 1970.

Army and Navy pensioners with emphasis on Civil and War of 1812 veterans.

United States. Record and Pension Office. *List of Libraries, Organizations and Educational Institutions in the Several States and Territories of the U.S. Supplied with the Official Records of the Union and Confederate Armies*. Washington, D.C.: 1903.

United States. War Department. *Pension Roll of 1835*. Report of the Secretary of War. U.S. Senate Document 514, 23rd Congress. 4 vols. Reprint. Baltimore: Genealogical Publishing Co., 1968.

d. Military Cemeteries.

The United States military dead are buried in cemeteries of four general types: temporary military cemeteries, permanent military cemeteries, national cemeteries, and army posts and other cemeteries. Records of the military dead are retained at the National Archives and Records Service, Washington, D.C.

United States. National Archives and Records Service. Record Group 92 Quartermaster Department.

Alphabetical Index to Places of Interment of Deceased Union Soldiers, 1868.

United States. National Archives. Record Group 92. Quartermaster Department.

Register of Confederate Soldiers, Sailors, and

Citizens Who Died in Federal Prisons and Military Hospitals in the North, 1861-1865.

United States. National Archives. Record Group 92. Quartermaster Department. Roll of Honor, 1865-1871. 27 vols.

Entries are arranged by name of cemetery and alphabetically by name of soldier.

e. Confederate Military Records

Brewer, James H. *The Confederate Negro: Virginia's Craftsmen and Military Laborers, 1861-1865*. Durham, N.C.: Duke University Press, 1969.

Focuses on blacks who worked for the Confederacy during the Civil War.

Confederate and Federal Papers, 1865. (TeSL)

Collection contains papers and personal materials; war death and cemetery records.

Confederate States of America, 1861-1865. (SCU)

Work and payroll records of blacks who worked for the Confederacy.

Record Group 109. War Department Collection of Confederate Records. National Archives.

Medical records for Mobile, Alabama, and register of patients; registers of civilians and blacks hired at Mobile including slaves; compiled records of Treasury Department and property claims; Quartermaster General's payroll of services; Medical Department. Ordinance, Macon, Ga., records for slaves hired and returns to owners. Regiments, battalions, and companies of Kentucky troops, including a list of black cooks. Bureau of Conscription, Virginia, 1864-1865; Farmville, Va., Hospital Records.

Tennessee Confederate Pension Applications, 1891. (TeSL)

Personal and family history for black and white veterans.

5. Federal Courts.

Record Group 21, Records of District Courts of the United States. (NAr and FARC, Chicago)

U.S. District Court Records, 1789-1959 for Region 5, with some records dealing with the slave trade.

Record Group 21, Records of District Courts of the United States. (NAr)

Includes District of Columbia records relating to slaves, 1851-1863; fugitive slave cases; records of the Board of Commissioners for the Emancipation of Slaves in the District of Columbia, 1862-1863; manumission and emancipation records for the District of Columbia, 1821-1862.

Record Group 21, Southern District of New York and Eastern District of Pennsylvania. (NAr)

Records including criminal matters relating to the slave trade dating from 1789 and civil matters from Reconstruction to 1912.

United States District Court, Kansas. Slave Compensation Case Files, 1866-1867. (NAr and FARC, Kansas)

Copies of claims filed by slave owners from the state of Missouri for compensation for services of slaves who were enlisted in the United States Army during the Civil War.

U.S. Second District Court. Burke County, Georgia. Slave List for 1798. (GaAr)

6. Penal Institutions.

MacNeil Island Federal Penitentiary, Washington State. Commitment Logs, 1891-1951.

"Records of Prisoners Received;" entries indicate personal description of prisoner and Afro-American prisoners are designated, "Negro." Personal data include birth date, parents and spouse's name, occupation, and religion. (NAr)

7. Miscellaneous Records.

Record Group 45, Naval Records Collection of the Office of Naval Records and Library. (NAr)

Logbooks of an African squadron including a list of slaves employed at Charleston, South Carolina, 1862-64.

Record Group 217, General Accounting Office.

Records of the Board of Commissioners for the emancipation of slaves in the District of Columbia, 1862-1863. (NAr)

Record Group 217, Records of the United States General Accounting Office (NAr)

South Carolina Direct Tax Commission certificate for land sold to Afro-American heads of families, 1863-1865; state and county records.

Record Group 217, Records of the United States General Accounting Office. (NAr)

Office of the Comptroller and Auditors payments to Afro-American troops, 1863-1865; Freedmen's Bureau accounts, 1867-1882; Navy payments to Afro-American soldiers.

United States Department of Labor. *List of Documents Pertaining to Black Workers among the Records of the Department of Labor and Its Component Bureaus, 1902-1969*. (NAr)

B. CITY, COUNTY, AND STATE RECORDS
1. General References
2. Registers and Lists
3. Population Reports and References
4. Court Records
   a. Deeds
   b. Wills
   c. Manumissions
   d. Bills of Sale
   e. Voter Registration Lists
   f. Marriage and Cohabitation Records
   g. Divorce Records
   h. Other Court Records
5. Vital Records: Births and Deaths
   a. Birth Records
   b. Death Records
6. City and County Directories
7. Tax Records
8. Other Records
9. Public Cemeteries
10. Agencies and Institutions
   a. Education Institutions
   b. Penal Institutions
   c. Welfare Agencies
   d. Medical Records
11. Other Records

1. General References.

Brewer, Mary Marie. *Index to Census Schedules in Printed Form; Those Avaialble and Where to Find Them.* Huntsville, Ark.: Century Enterprises, 1969.

A listing by state and county of early published censuses with indication of availability and price.

Day, John. *Descriptive Inventory of the Archives of the City and County of Philadelphia.* Phila.: The author, 1970.

This work lists innumerable sources of the archives of the city and county of Philadelphia.

Kirkman, E. Kay. *The Counties of the United States, Their Derivation and Census Schedules*. Salt Lake City, Utah: The author, 1971.

Peterson, Clarence Stewart, compiler. *Consolidated Bibliography of County Histories in Fifty States in 1961*. Baltimore: 1961. Reprint. Baltimore: Genealogical Publishing Co., 1963.

Aims to list all county histories of 100 pages or more.

United States. Library of Congress. Library Census Project. *State Census: An Annotated Bibliography of Censuses of Population Taken after the Year 1790 by State and Territories in the United States*. Washington, D.C.: GPO, 1948.

United States. Works Projects Administration. *Inventory of County Archives of Pennsylvania*. Gettysburg: Pennsylvania Historical Records Survey, 1941.

———. *List of Vital Statistical Records*. Washington, D.C.: GPO, 1943.

A state-by-state compilation of the whereabouts of marriage, birth, and death records compiled by WPA workers in the 1930s.

2. Registers and Lists

Burke County, Georgia
Slave List, 1798. (GaAr)

Clark County, Indiana.
Register of Negroes, 1805-10 (IndSL)

Clay County, Missouri
Freed Negro Registry, 1836-56. (IndSL)

Fayette County, Pennsylvania.
Negro Birth Register, 1788-1826.

This register includes names of slaves, slave-owners, dates of birth, and name of child and parents.

Franklin County, Georgia.
Register, 1852. (IndSL)

This list includes persons designated as Negroes and mulattoes.

Gates County, North Carolina.
Registration of slaves to work on Great Dismal Swamp, 1847-61. Raleigh, N.C.: North Carolina State Archives, 1974.

Haller, Stephen E., and Robert H. Smith, Jr. *Register of Blacks in the Miami Valley (Ohio), a Name Abstract, 1804-57*. Dayton, Ohio: Wright State University, 1977. (ALPLI)

Lancaster County, Pennsylvania.
Slave Register, 1790-1888. (IndSL)

This register lists names and addresses of owners of slaves, names of slave mothers and children and their dates of birth, sex, age, and dates of manumission.

Martin County, Indiana.
Negro Register, 1853. (IndSL)

List includes a description of all Negroes in the county.

Morgan County, Georgia. Ordinary Court.
Slave Register, 1812-24. (GaAr)

New Jersey Abolition Society.
List of Afro-Americans in South New Jersey Towns, 1798-99. (GbSC)

Pulaski County, Georgia. Ordinary Court.
Slave Records. (GaAr)

Register of Negro Slaves and Masters for 1805-07, Knox County, Indiana Territory. Chicago: Barrackman Family Association, 1970. (ALPLI)

Richmond County, Georgia. Superior Court.
Slave Requisition, 1818-20; 1822-30; 1835-37. (GaAr)

Savannah, Georgia.
Register of Free Persons of Color, 1817-29; 1860-63. (GaAr, GaHS)

Warren County, Georgia. Superior Court.
Slave Owner's List, 1798. (GaAr)

3. Population Reports and References.
Special population censuses are taken from time to

time by cities, states, and counties and they include general as well as selected population focuses. Studies and analyses of population reports and data are also written and compiled by private individuals as well as public agencies.

California.
Special Census of Selected Cities, 1897-1938. (CaAr)

This census includes names in alphabetical order including age, sex, color and occupation of person.

Columbia, Missouri. Social and Economic Census of the Colored Population, 1901. (ALPLI)

This census consists of family reports listing members with ages, income, and living condition.

Early Delaware Census Records, 1665-1697. Steeples Bountiful, Utah: Accelerated Indexing Systems, Inc., 1977. (DelHS)

4. Court Records

Court records include civil (private) and criminal (public) matters. The courts, set up under statute, differ from state to state. Attempts to distinguish between state and federal courts can be time consuming because many of the courts have the same names. Court records are of genealogical value and include wills, deeds, complaints, answers, summons, subpoenas, orders, judgements, decrees, injunctions, petitions, motions, depositions, pleadings, sentences, decrees, and all proceedings and testimony of every case detailed in court records. Court records more often used in Afro-American genealogy are illustrated by examples in this Section. These include deeds, wills, manumissions, bills of sale, marriage and cohabitation bonds, divorce, and registrations. Some states and counties maintain records predating the Civil War that are housed in collections known as "Slavery Records." These collections include a variety of types of court records. Some counties still maintain these records, while others have been removed to the archives of the state. James Rose and Alice Eichholz' *Black Genesis* includes a state-by-state listing of court records involving blacks in the southern states prior to 1865. Some general references to court records include:

Catterall, Helen Honor Turncliff. *Judicial Cases Concerning American Slavery and the Negro.*

Ardery, Julia Hope. *Kentucky Court and Other Records.* v. 2, *Kentucky Records, 1932.* Reprint. Baltimore: Genealogical Publishing, 1972.

McBee, May Wilson, comp. *Mississippi County Court Records, 1958.* Reprint. Baltimore: Genealogical Publishing, 1967.

a. Deeds.

A deed is a document by which title in real property is transferred from one party to another. Deeds are of interest to Afro-Americans for two major reasons: (1) information regarding the transfer and receipt of real property, and description and value of the property, and (2) information regarding human beings, such as a slave, who was transferred from one party to another in treatment as property. Information on the deed includes the parties of the deed, the places of residence of the parties, the consideration involved in the price, and the description of the property. Description of human beings as property may include the name of the slave, age (approximate if not actual), sex of the individual, special skills, and distinguishing features (hair color, color of eyes, scars, etc.).

Record of the transaction of a deed is generally maintained with the recorder of deeds in the county of the event. Copies of deeds may be found among private papers of individuals and in estate papers in various agencies.

Delaware. New Castle, Kent, and Sussex Counties.
Probate Records, 1700-1900 (DelHS)

Probate records include deeds with names of blacks listed in them.

Jackson, Michael
Deed of Emancipation, November 12, 1798. (IndHS)

This deed sets two female slaves free.

Jones County, Georgia. Superior Court.
Index to Slave Deeds, 1791-1864. (GaAr)

Mississippi. Adams-Yazoo Counties.
Deeds, 1817-1865.

Collection contains scattered references to "freedmen."

Smith, Elizabeth. Lincoln County, Kentucky. July 14, 1796. (IndSL)

Deed for five slaves: Elizabeth Smith to John and Thomas Smith.

See also indexes to deeds in "Basic Reference Sources" of this book.

b. Wills.

A will is the declaration of a person's desires concerning the disposition of his/her property after his/her death. Information relating to wills include the executors, administrators, guardians and curators, property inventories, and appraisals and inheritance tax receipts. Wills establish relationships through identification of names, dates, and locations and verification of death dates. Wills have unique value to the Afro-American genealogy searcher. Dispositions of slaves as "property" are common in the wills of former slaveholders. Many of the wills manumitted or set the slave free; some willed that the slave should have certain real properties; while still others directed who was to receive the slave. Often a family member inherited a slave. Some wills indicate that a slave was to be sold to pay off any remaining debts owed by the decedent.

Wills, as deeds, are records of the probate court. Other agencies have copies of wills. These include the collections of historical and genealogical societies, state archives, the National Archives, the Library of Congress, and special collections of colleges and universities.

Colonial Dames of America, Delaware. Historical Reserve Committee. *A Calendar of Delaware Wills. New Castle County, 1628-1800*. New Castle County: 1911. Reprint. Baltimore: Genealogical Publishing, 1969.

Daughters of the American Revolution. *Index to Alabama Wills, 1808-1870*. Baltimore: Genealogical Publishing, 1955.

This source is an index to wills of slaveholders.

Hershkowitz, Leo. *Wills of Early New York Jews, 1704-1799*. New York: American Jewish Historical Society, 1967.

Contains a list of forty-eight wills and the names of blacks listed in them.

Magruder, J.M. *Index of Maryland Colonial Wills, 1634-1777 in the Halls of Records, Annapolis, Maryland*. Annapolis, Maryland. 1933. Reprint, 3 vols. in 1. Baltimore: Genealogical Publishing, 1967.

North Carolina. Secretary of State. *Abstracts of North Carolina Wills Compiled from Original and Recorded Wills in the Office of the Secretary of State*. Compiled by J. Bryan Crimes. N.C.: 1910. Reprint. Baltimore: Genealogical Publishing, 1975.

c. Manumissions.

A manumission paper is a formal statement that a slave has been granted freedom. These records appear in different forms and may be a part of a will or a separate document. These documents may be found as a part of public records or in the possession of private families. Libraries and special collections noted for maintaining manuscript collections of early American residents or slaveholders include the University of Virginia, Duke University, the University of North Carolina, the Pennsylvania State Historical Society, the Library of Congress, and the National Archives.

Alfred, Terry L. "Some Manumissions Recorded on the Adams County Deed Books in Chancery Clerk's Office, Natchez, Mississippi, 1795-1835." *Journal of Mississippi History*. 33(No. 1, February 1971): 39-50.

Connecticut Historical Society. Manumissions, 1751-1861.

These records are contained in the Slavery Documents Collection of the Society.

New Jersey (State) Archives and Records Management. Manumissions Records, 1788-1853; 1804-1862.

An 1804 law of New Jersey required all male slaves born after July 4, 1804, reaching age 25, and all female slaves reaching age 21 to be manumitted. Original records are retained by the County Court Clerk offices.

Pennsylvania Abolition Society.
Manumission of Slaves and Indentures of Servants, 1748-1868. (PeHS)

Identification of slave manumission is in these records by specific owner's name and distinct name of plantations.

Yoshpe, Harry B. "Records of Slave Manumissions in New York." *Journal of Negro History*. 26 (1941): 78-107.

(See: Helen Honor Catterall, *Judicial Cases American Slavery and the Negro* for lists of hundreds of manumissions.)

Also refer to plantation records under Private Resources for further indications of slave manumissions.

d. Bills of Sale.

A bill of sale indicates a transfer of ownership by sale. A bill of sale is more often cited as a land record although not all sales involve the transfer of land. Because slaves were considered property, the buying and selling of these people were frequently recorded in land record books. Bills of sales of slaves can be found in collections of private papers, among plantation records, and in records of slave trading and traders.

Albany County, New York. Office of the Secretary of State.

Assorted records on slaves including bills of sale.

Connecticut Historical Society.
Slavery Documents Collection, 1751-1861.

Collection includes numerous bills of sale.

Delaware Historical Society.
Scattered records of New Castle, Kent, and Sussex Counties, Delaware, 1733-1857.

Collection includes bills of sales and other transactions of slavery.

COLORED VOLUNTEER ENLISTMENT.

State of Missouri Town of Tipton

I, Albert Cavanaugh born in Cooper Co. in the State of Missouri aged 30 years, and by occupation a Farmer Do HEREBY ACKNOWLEDGE to have volunteered this 11th day of January 1864, to serve as a Soldier in the Army of the United States of America, for the period of THREE YEARS, unless sooner discharged by proper authority: Do also agree to accept such bounty, pay, rations, and clothing, as are, or may be, established by law for Colored Volunteers. And I, Albert Cavanaugh do solemnly swear, that I will bear true faith and allegiance to the UNITED STATES OF AMERICA, and that I will serve them honestly and faithfully against all their enemies or opposers whomsoever; and that I will observe and obey the orders of the President of the United States, and the orders of the officers appointed over me, according to the Rules and Articles of War.

Albert his X mark Cavanaugh

Sworn and subscribed to at Tipton Missouri
this 11th *day of* January 1864
BEFORE Franklin Swap Lt. & Pro. Mar.

This "volunteer" was a slave whose owner submitted him in substitute for his service. The owner applied for compensation for the service of the slave.

See also plantation records under Private Resources for additional indications of bills of sale in manuscript collections.

e. Voter Registration Lists

Voter registration lists are generated in county agencies. Early lists may be removed to the state archives.

Decatur, Georgia. Superior Court.
Voter Registration, 1902. (GaAr)

Los Angeles County, California.
Black voters, 1892, 1896, 1898.

Includes black male voters' names and map indicating voters' residences and changes in occupation.

Marion County, Georgia. Superior Court. Voter Lists, 1898, 1900, 1903, 1906. (GaAr)

McDuffie County, Georgia. Ordinary Court.
Voter Registration, 1896-1904. (GaAr)

Texas State.
Voter Registration, 1867. (TxSL)

Following the Civil War, the Reconstruction government required all persons wishing to be refranchised to register to vote and to take a loyalty oath. Efforts were made to register as many freedmen as possible. Ledgers available for all the existing counties at that time include name, length of residence in state, county and precinct, and place of birth.

United States. Works Projects Administration.
Index to Inumeration of Male Voters of Miami County, Indiana, 1850-1920. (IndSL)

f. Marriage and Cohabitation Records.

Marriage records appear quite early in U.S. history. While genealogical information in the early records is limited, later records are more detailed. Most marriage records are kept in the county where the marriage license was issued. Many family Bibles list the names and dates of marriages of family members and places where the marriages transpired. Marriage records and sources of information may also be found among census records, church records, Freedmen's Bureau records, newspaper announcements, township and war records, manuscript collections, and private family collections.

Free Afro-Americans prior to the Civil War could be legally married, and the records of these marriages in all parts of the country are found in the traditional public records. More such records can be found in the north and northeast rather than the slaveholding states. Some counties in the south prior to 1865 maintained record groups called "*slaves and free men of color*," and a number of types of records can be found in these collections.

For the black person in bondage, marriage was not a legally binding matter and was often treated as a farce. *Marriage* rituals included "*Jumping over a broomstick*" and "*marrying in the blanket*." Other rituals included the reading of the Bible, singing of songs, a statement read by a *preacher*, and a simple "*yes*" from both parties. These marriage customs, however, were not confined to blacks but also were practiced some by poor whites. Couples took these rituals seriously, and many who survived separation by sales and relocations *cohabitated* as man and wife for many years.

Slaves who were married by one ritual or another but without legal sanction and who lived as man and wife for a number of years could in some states, upon Emancipation, apply to the court of the county for a *cohabitation bond*, a certificate that legalized the union of the couple. North Carolina is one of the southern states that has developed an index of the names of freed men who applied for and were issued cohabitation bonds.

Black Marriage Records of Fayette County, Kentucky, 1886-1876. Lexington, Ky.: Kentucky Tree Search, [1985]

This work includes the first three volumes of marriages of *People of Color* registered in Fayette County, Kentucky Courthouse.

Everly, Elaine C. "Marriage Records of Freedmen." *Prologue: The Journal of the National Archives*. 5 (Spring 1973): 150-54.

Georgia. Department of Archives and History. Vital Records.

Records document marriages of blacks dating from 1823.

Jackson, Catherine A. "An Index to Marriage Bonds Filed in the North Carolina State Archives." *Archives Information Circulation* No. 15. Raleigh: North Carolina Department of Archives and History.

Love, Edgar F. "Marriage Patterns of Persons of African Descent in Colonial Mexico in a Colonial Mexico City Parish." *Hispanic American Historic Review*. 5(1979): 79-91.

Marriages among thousands of Afro-Americans who migrated from the U.S. between 1865-1875 are discussed.

North Carolina. Department of Archives and History, Raleigh.

Archives has the Cohabitation and Marriage Records for Roberson County 1850-1866. Cohabitation records are also available for the following counties: Edgecomb, Forsyth, Franklin, Granville, New Hanover, Orange, Pasquotank, Person, Pitt, Rowan, Stokes, Wake.

Archives has marriage records of blacks dating from 1848. Records also on microfilm at Allen County Public Library, Fort Wayne, Indiana.

United States. Department of Health, Education and Welfare. *Where to Write for Marriage Records in the United States and Outlying Areas*. Public Health Service Publication No. 630B. Washington, D.C.: Public Health Service.

United States. Works Projects Administration. *Inventories of County Archives, Church Archives, Vital Statistics Records, etc.*, Published by the various states as the *Historical Records Survey* (under dates of the 1930s and 1940s).

g. Divorce Records.

In most states of the nation, the court has the authority to grant divorces and control other equity matters. Genealogical information in court records includes the name of the couple who was divorced, date and place of birth of both parties, and date and place of marriage. Names of children of the marriage will appear in the court records but not on the divorce certificate. Records of divorces are kept in the courts and are open to the public.

Courts with Authority to Grant Divorces
by state

Alabama	Circuit Court in the county.
Alaska	Superior (there are four districts).
Arizona	Superior Court in the county.
Arkansas	County Chancery Court.
California	County Superior Court.
Colorado	District Court in the county.
Connecticut	Superior Court in the county.
Delaware	Superior Court in the county.
District of Columbia	Court of General Sessions.
Florida	Circuit Court in the county.
Georgia	Superior Court in the county.
Hawaii	Circuit court.
Idaho	District Court in the county.
Illinois	Circuit Court in the county.
Indiana	Circuit Court in the county or Superior Court in the county.
Iowa	District Court in the county.
Kansas	District Court in the county.
Kentucky	Circuit Court in the county.
Louisiana	District Court in the parish.
Maine	Superior Court in the county.
Maryland	Circuit Court in the county.
Massachusetts	County Probate Court and Superior Court in the county have concurrent jurisdiction.
Michigan	Circuit Court in the county.
Minnesota	District Court in the county.
Mississippi	Chancery Court in the county.
Missouri	Circuit Court in the county.
Montana	District Court in the county.
Nebraska	District Court in the county.
Nevada	District Court in the county.
New Hampshire	Superior Court in the county.
New Jersey	District Court in the county.
New Mexico	District Court in the county.
New York	County Court.

North Carolina	Superior Court in the county.
North Dakota	District Court in the county.
Ohio	Court of Common Pleas in the county.
Oklahoma	District Court in the county and Superior Court in the county have concurrent jurisdiction.
Oregon	Circuit Court in the county.
Pennsylvania	Court of Common Pleas in the county.
Rhode Island	Family Court in the county (Prior to the Family Court, the Superior Court in county handled divorces).
South Carolina	County Court (Divorce in South Carolina was not legal prior to 1949).
South Dakota	Circuit Court in the county.
Tennessee	Circuit Court in the county and Chancery Court in the county have concurrent jurisdiction.
Texas	District Court in the county.
Utah	District Court in the county.
Vermont	County Court.
Virginia	Any court with equity jurisdiction (Usually County Circuit Court cities also have courts with jurisdiction.)
Washington	Family Court (This court is a department of the County Superior Court.)
West Virginia	Circuit Court in the county (except in the counties where there are Domestic Relations Courts).
Wisconsin	County Court and Circuit Court in the county have concurrent jurisdiction (except in Milwaukee where Circuit Court has sole jurisdiction).
Wyoming	District Court in the county.

From Val D. Greenwood. *The Researcher's Guide to American Genealogy*. (Baltimore: Genealogical Publishing, 1978).

h. Other Court Records

Baldwin County, Georgia. Inferior Court Minutes. Trials of Slaves, 1812-1838; 1812-1826. (GaAr)

Elbert County, Georgia. Inferior Court. Slave Trials, 1837-1849. (GaAr)

Georgia. Inferior Court. County Records of Georgia.
Trials of Slaves, 1812. (GaAr)

Hancock County, Georgia. Inferior Court. Slave Trials, 1834-1850. (GaAr)

Lincoln County, Georgia. Inferior Court. Docket of Slaves Indicted for Capital Crimes, 1814-1838. (GaAr)

Screven County, Georgia. Inferior Court. Docket for Trials of Slaves and Free Persons of Color, 1844-1848. (GaAr)

See also B.2, this Section for Registers and Lists of the Courts.

5. Vital Records: Births and Deaths

Vital records are primarily public civil records of births, deaths, marriages, and divorce. Private agencies, especially the church, have maintained these records. In early years before the development of public records, baptismal records, marriage rites, and records of deaths and burials were largely the domain of the church. In the United States vital record keeping has been largely a state responsibility, and as a result each state has developed its own system of registration under the prodding and direction of the federal government.

In 1850 the federal population census reflected innovations in federal census taking and inaugurated vital registration information. In 1860 a column was added to the federal population schedules to record the month of birth for those born in the census year. The census as a tool for collecting vital records was not abandoned until 1910, when the states showed sufficient evidence that they had developed a more effective system for gathering and recording vital statistics.

Since 1910 it has been a relatively easy matter to locate and secure copies of vital records.

Prior to 1865 public records on births, deaths, and marriages of blacks in the slaveholding states were limited. Marriage records were largely confined to free blacks. Births and death records were largely confined to plantation records unless the black person was free. Free blacks more often are included in public records. However, many states maintained these records among such collections as "slaves and free persons of color." Therefore, vital statistics for Afro-Americans can be found in both public and private records. And for those persons born before 1865, plantation records, family Bibles, and church records are the more likely sources for persons who lived in the southern states.

Cohabitation records have been established for some states for those persons who lived together as man and wife under existing codes of marriage during slavery. Upon emancipation, some states, such as North Carolina, allowed these persons to file for cohabitation bonds.

Most county courthouses today retain vital records. In some areas the county board of health as well as the state board of health maintains records of births and deaths. Earlier records may be housed in the state library or archives.

Vital records of marriages are treated under Court Records in this section.

a. Birth Records.

Uniform registration of births in the United States was attempted after 1810. The last states to adopt statewide birth and death records were Georgia and New Mexico that did so in 1919.

Local agencies have kept various records for many years in many forms under various headings. Some counties and states in the north and south have registers of *Negro* births. Records of births of free Afro-Americans before 1865 may be found in public records in both the north and south with some of the records being listed among *Slaves and free persons of color* and in general records with designations of race.

Examples of early birth records for Afro-Americans include:

Fayette County, Pennsylvania.
Negro Birth Register, 1788-1826. (PeAr)

Includes name of slave owner, dates of birth, and names of child and parents.

Hendrix, Mary Flowers. "Birth, Deaths and Aged Persons for Claiburne County, 1822," *Journal of Mississippi History*. 16 (1954): 37-46.

New Jersey (State)
Birth Records, June 1848-1878. (NJArRM)

Births are sometimes designated by race.

Other sources useful in determining the availability and location of birth records are Sargent B. Child and Dorothy P. Holmes, *Check List of Historical Records Survey Publications: Bibliography of Research Projects Reports*. Reprint. Baltimore: Genealogical Publishing Co., 1969.

Where to Write for Births and Deaths of U.S. Citizens Who Were Born or Died outside the United States for Alien Children Adopted by U.S. Citizens. (Public Health Service Publication No. 630A-2) and *Where to Write for Birth and Death Records, United States and Outlying Areas*. (Public Health Service Publication No. 630A-1)

b. Death Records

Records of certificates of death may be secured from the agency in the state that maintains vital statistics. Other sources of such records are the hospital where a person died and the office of the medical examiner or coroner. Funeral directors may have copies of death certificates. Aids in locating records of deaths include the United States Public Health Service's publication *Where to Write for Birth and Death Records*. (See Birth Records, 5.a of this section.)

Death records, like birth records, are in more complete forms in the New England states, especially for the earlier years.

For a list of agencies that maintain vital statistics, including death records, see the section on Directory of Resources.

6. City and County Directories.

Chicago, Illinois. City Directories, 1880, 1890, 1900, 1910, 1917. (FARCC)

Connecticut. City Directories, 1838- (CnHS)

For some years Afro-American residents were listed in a separate section.

Indianapolis, Indiana. City Directories, 1849- (IndSL)

All city and county directories are available. Notation of race is not consistently made but may be found in several directories.

New York (State) City and County Directories. (NYSL)

A collection of several thousand directories. Nineteenth-century directories use the designation, "col."

Philadelphia, Pennsylvania. City Directories, 1795-1935 (PeHS)

San Francisco, California. City Directories. 1875- (CaSLSu)

Designations by color prior to 1875.

Most cities have directories and these may be found at the local public library, local college and university, and the state library or archives.

Telephone directories are available for areas where telephones are available. Early volumes of telephone directories may be found in similar places as city directories, as well as with the local telephone company.

7. Tax Records.

Tax records are a widely recognized and important source of genealogical information. There are varying kinds of tax records including real property and personal property. Citizens in the states have paid and continue to pay a variety of types of taxes. An 1875 Marshal County, Tennessee, tax record lists individuals who paid "railroad" and "school" taxes. Tax records are of interest to the Afro-American genealogist for two major reasons: identification of an ancestor who paid taxes and an ancestor on whom tax was paid. The county courthouse and the public and private libraries that maintain microfilm copies of early tax rolls are initial sources of tax records information.

Atlanta, Georgia
Tax Digest, 1859-1867; 1869. (GaAr)

Norris, Garland C. *Tax List of Culpepper County, Virginia and Names of Slaves, 1783*. Raleigh, N.C.: G.C. Norris. (ALPLI)

Paterson, Trenton, and other Municipalities.
Tax Rolls, 1880s-1900s. (NJArRM)

Watson, Alan D. "The Colonial Tax List." *North Carolina Genealogical Society Journal*, 15 (November 1979): 218-45.

Slaves are often listed by name and tables contain designations of race.

Wellman, Manly Wade. *The County of Warren, North Carolina, 1856-1917*. Chapel Hill, N.C.: University of North Carolina Press, 1959.

Includes persons taxable in the county in 1781 with names of slaveholders.

8. Other Records.

Connecticut (State)
Town Meeting Records. (CnHS)

Town clerks offices' maintained records of cases of Afro-Americans who filed suits or were subjects as paupers.

9. Public Cemeteries

Public cemeteries are owned and operated by an agency of government and are maintained by public funds. Military cemeteries are treated separately in this work. These records may be found in the National Archives, archives of the states, and some records may be held by such organizations as the Daughters of the American Revolution. Agencies that are helpful in locating cemeteries include the National Archives, state libraries and archives and local chambers of commerce, funeral directors, and the reference, *United States Government Genealogical Survey of Maps of Locality*.

American Blue Book of Funeral Directors. New York: National Funeral Directors Association (Biennial).

This publication is a useful source in locating a

funeral director who may have records or information on a burial in a specific cemetery.

Day, John. "Cemetery Returns, 1803-06," in *Descriptive Inventory of the Archives of the City and County of Philadelphia*. Philadelphia: The author, 1970.

Afro-Americans are listed in this source and designated by a "B."

Georgia State Archives.
Cemetery Records:
Central State Hospital, 1800-1851.
Laurel Grove Cemetery (Chatham County), 1852-1942.
Oak Grove Cemetery (Sumter County), 1903-1959.
Old Negro Cemetery (Thomas County)

Mississippi. Department of Archives and History.
Cemetery Records, 1862-1938.

Records of burials at Greenwood (City) Cemetery, Jackson, Mississippi, 1823-1860; lots sold, 1862-1915; roster of cemeteries in Monroe County with indexes of family names.

National Funeral directors and Morticians Association, Inc. Chicago, Illinois.

Lists names of black funeral directors throughout the United States and some Caribbean nations.

New York (State) Library
Church and Cemetery Records.

The State Library of New York has an extensive collection of cemetery records predating 1880 when the state did not keep vital records. Includes both public and private cemeteries.

North Carolina. Department of Archives and History.
Indexes to Tombstones.

The Archives maintains an index to inscriptions on tombstones found in cemeteries in all counties in North Carolina. This project was undertaken by personnel provided through the Works Project Administration of the 1930s and includes public and private cemeteries.

10. Agencies and Institutions

Records of public education include the public schools, colleges and universities, and special agencies serving education. Records include transactions of public affairs affecting the schools, papers and memorabilia of students, faculty, and benefactors to education, registration, and application records. Black colleges and universities have resources that are yet to be fully tapped.

a. Education Institutions

Examples of education resources include:

Atwood, Rufus B., 1897-1983.
Papers. (KeSCF)

Speeches, addresses, photographs of the former president of Kentucky State University, 1929-1962.

Crispus Attucks High School. Indianapolis, Indiana.
Yearbooks, 1955 and uneven years. (IndSL)

Fayette County Georgia.
School Census, 1928, 1933, 1938. (GaAr)

Meriwether County, Georgia. Superintendent of Schools. School Census, 1898, 1903, 1913. (GaAr)

North Carolina. Department of Public Instruction. Division of Negro Education.
Records of the Division of Negro Education, 1900-1961. (NCAr)

Includes correspondences relating to teacher education, Indian education, and the development of black colleges.

Tennessee State Library and Archives.
Records of the Nashville Public Schools.

Other sources that may be consulted include the Boston Public Library, Anti-Slavery Collection which includes letters and manuscripts relating to Freedmen's schools and the Freedmen's Bureau, Record Groups including school reports.

b. Penal Institutions.

California. Department of Corrections Records, 1850-1940. (CaAr)

The San Quentin and Folsom State Prisons records include prison registers, case files, photo albums, and pardon and commitment papers alphabetically arranged by inmates' names since 1930.

Mississippi. Adams-Yazoo Counties.
Prison Records, 1855-1930. (MsDAR)

Prison records are identified by race.

New Jersey. Trenton State Prison.
Accounts, Register, Inventories, etc., of the Trenton State Prison, 1798-1841. (NJArRM)

New Jersey. Rahway State Prison.
Prison records including examinations, physical descriptions, statements and photographs of Rahway State Prison, New Jersey, 1902-47. (NJarRM)

Wyoming State Prison. Records, 1873-1970. (WyAr)

Where description of inmate is noted, race is indicated.

c. Welfare Agencies

California.
State Agency Records for Social Welfare and Social Services Departments. (Years vary) (CaAr)

New York County.
Association for the Benefit of Colored Orphans, New York County, New York, 1836-present.

Includes names of more than 10,000 children and some parents; indenture records; admission, discharges; visitors, births, deaths, and marriages.

North Carolina. Department of Public Welfare.
Consultant for Negro Work.
Records, 1925-1960 (NCAr)

Records include pictures of inmates, employment records; black teacher's association; training of black social workers.

Philadelphia, Pennsylvania.
Register of Children's Asylum, 1819-1887.
9 vols. (PeHS)

Spears, Jean E., and Dorothy Paul.
Admission Records, Indianapolis Asylum for Friendless Colored Children, 1871-1900. Indianapolis, Indiana: Indiana Historical Society, 1978. (ALPLI)

d. Medical Records

Good Samaritan Hospital, Charlotte, North Carolina.
Records, 1891-1960. (NCAr)

The first hospital in the United States built and operated exclusively for Afro-Americans. Organized under the auspices of St. Peter Episcopal Church, the hospital was private until 1960 when it was given to the city of Charlotte.

Mississippi. Adams, Hicks, and Warren Counties.
Medical Records, 1880-1940. (MsDAR)

Records include annual reports and other records of county medical and health care agencies.

(See also *Medical and Surgical History of the War of Rebellion*, Part III, Section A.4.b.4 for names of Afro-American patients and their regiments.)

11. Other Records

Articles of Incorporation, 1850-1960. (CaAr)

Includes purposes, place of business, stock involved, and person who directed the company. Records differentiate companies as "black" or "colored."

California. Board of Medical Examiners.
Professional and Vocational Standards, 1901-1968. (CaAr)

Separated by ethnic groups, records are alphabetically arranged under headings including "deceased physicians files."

Texas.
Memorials and Petitions, 1836-1845. (TxSL)

Occasionally free blacks would petition the legislature for a specific reason. Records are indexed by name of individual submitting the petition.

PART IV

DIRECTORY OF RESOURCES

A. SOURCES FOR VITAL STATISTICS: BIRTHS, DEATHS, AND MARRIAGES
B. PUBLIC LIBRARIES
   1. State Libraries and Archives
   2. Libraries Serving Predominantly Black Communities
C. SOME MAJOR COLLECTIONS AND LIBRARIES FOR GENEALOGY RESEARCH
D. HISTORICALLY BLACK COLLEGES AND UNIVERSITIES
E. SOME GENEALOGICAL AND HISTORICAL SOCIETIES AND ORGANIZATIONS
F. KEY TO LOCATION SYMBOLS

A. SOURCES FOR VITAL STATISTICS; BIRTHS, DEATHS, AND MARRIAGES

Alabama. Bureau of Vital Statistics
State Department of Public Health
Montgomery, AL 36104

(Birth and deaths date from 1908; marriages, from 1936. Records are also with probate court of each county.)

Alabama Mobile County Board of Health
P.O. Box 4533
Mobile, AL 36604

(Births date from 1871; deaths from 1820)

Alaska. State Department of Health and Welfare
Bureau of Vital Statistics
State Office Building
Juneau, AK 99801

(Records date from 1913)

Arizona. State Board of Health.
Bureau of Vital Statistics
Phoenix, AZ 85007

Arkansas. State Department of Health
Bureau of Vital Statistics
4815 W. Markham Street
Little Rock, AR 72201

(Records of births and deaths date from 1914; marriages, 1917)

California. State Department of Public Health.
Bureau of Vital Statistics and Data Processing
631 J Street
Sacramento, CA 95814

(Birth and death records date from 1905; marriage records are kept by county clerks and date from 1905.)

Colorado. State Department of Health.
Records and Statistics Section
4210 E. 11th Avenue
Denver, CO 80220

(Birth and death records date from 1910. Some records date to the 1860s; marriages from 1904.)

Connecticut. State Department of Health.
Public Health Statistics Section
79 Elm Street
Hartford, CT 06115

(Birth and death records date from 1897. Birth, death, and marriage records are also filed with each town clerk.)

Delaware. State Board of Health
Bureau of Vital Statistics
P.O. Box 637
Dover, DE 19901

(Birth and death records date from 1860; earlier records are with the justice of the peace in each county.)

District of Columbia. Department of Public Health
Vital Records Division
300 Indiana Avenue, NW
Washington, DC 20001

(Birth records date from 1871; death records from 1855; marriage records from 1811.)

Florida. State Department of Health
Bureau of Vital Statistics
P.O. Box 210
Jacksonville, FL 32201

(Birth records date from 1865; death records from 1877; marriage from 1927. Marriage records available from county judge in each county.)

Georgia. State Department of Public Health
Vital Records Service
47 Trinity Avenue, SW
Atlanta, GA 30334

Hawaii. State Department of Health
Research and Statistics Office
P.O. Box 3378
Honolulu, HI 96801

(Birth records date from 1850; death records from 1861; marriages from 1849.)

Idaho. State Department of Health
Bureau of Vital Statistics
Boise, ID 83707

(Birth, death, and marriage records from 1911. Marriage records are in county recorder's office for each county.)

Illinois. Department of Public Health
Bureau of Vital Statistics
525 W. Jefferson Street
Springfield, IL 62706

(Birth and death records from 1916. Marriage records in county clerk's office are from date of county's organization.)

Indiana. State Board of Health
1330 W. Michigan Street
Indianapolis, IN 43206

(Births from 1907; death records date from 1900, and marriage records from 1958. Early marriage records from 1882 to 1908 may be found in the office of the county clerk of each county or in the state archives in Indianapolis.)

Iowa. State Department of Health
Division of Records and Statistics
Des Moines, IA 50319

(Birth records 1880; deaths from 1896; marriages from 1916. Marriage records are in probate court for each county.)

Kansas. Division of Vital Statistics
Records Section
Topeka, KS 66612

Kentucky. State Department of Health
Office of Vital Statistics
27 E. Main Street
Frankfort, KY 40601

(Birth and death records from 1911; marriages from 1958. Earlier marriages can be found with each county clerk.)

Louisiana. State Department of Health
Division of Public Health Statistics
P.O. Box 60630
New Orleans, LA 70610

Maine. State Department of Health and Welfare
Office of Vital Statistics
State House
Augusta, ME 04330

(Birth, death, and marriage records date from 1892; earlier records may be found in offices of town clerk where event occurred.)

Maryland. State Department of Health
Division of Vital Statistics
State Office Building
301 W. Preston Street
Baltimore, MD 21201

(Birth and death records date from 1898; marriages from June 1951 for the entire state except for the city of Baltimore.)

Massachusetts. Office of the Secretary of State
Division of Vital Statistics
272 State House
Boston, MA 02133

(Birth, death, and marriage records date from 1841 for the entire state except for the city of Boston. Earlier records may be found in office of city or town clerk.)

Michigan. Department of Health
Vital Records Section
3500 N. Logan Street
Lansing, MI 48914

(Birth and death records date from 1867; marriages from 1868.)

Minnesota. State Department of Health
Section of Vital Statistics
350 State Office Building
St. Paul, MN 55101

(Birth and deaths from 1900; marriage records in custody of clerk of the district court in each county.)

Mississippi. State Board of Health
Vital Records Registration
P.O. Box 1700
Jackson, MS 39205

(Birth and death records date from 1912; marriage records from 1926 and are in custody of the clerk of the circuit court in each county.)

Missouri. Division of Health
Vital Records
State Department of Public Welfare
Jefferson City, MO 65101

(Birth and death records date from 1910; marriage records are in custody of recorder of deeds in each county.)

Montana. State Department of Health
Division of Records and Statistics
Helena, MT 59601

(Birth and death records date from 1907; marriages from 1943. Earlier marriage records date from organization of the county and are in custody of clerk of the court in each county.)

Nebraska. State Department of Health
Bureau of Vital Statistics
P.O. Box 94757
Lincoln, NB 68509

(Birth and death records date from 1904; marriages from 1909. Earlier records are in custody of county judge in each county.)

Nevada. Department of Health Welfare and Rehabilitation.
Division of Health
Section of Vital Statistics
Carson City, NV 89701

New Hampshire. State Department of Health and Welfare
Bureau of Vital Statistics
61 S. Spring Street
Concord, NH 03301

(Birth, death, and marriage records date from 1640. Town clerk has records.)

New Jersey. State Department of Health
Bureau of Vital Statistics
P.O. Box 1540
Trenton, NJ 08625

(Birth, death, and marriage records date from 1878; some early records date from 1665 to 1880 and are in the New Jersey archives.)

New Mexico. State Department of Health and Social Services
P.O. Box 2348
Sante Fe, NM 87501

(Birth and death records date from 1920. Write county clerk of each county for marriage records.)

New York. State Department of Health
Bureau of Vital Statistics
84 Holland Avenue
Albany, NY 12208

(Birth, death, and marriage records date from 1880 except for New York City, Albany, Buffalo, and Yonkers.)

North Carolina. State Board of Health
Office of Vital Statistics
P.O. Box 2091
Raleigh, NC 27602

(Birth records from 1913; death records from 1903 and marriages from 1962. Marriage records are in the office of the register of deeds in each county. Marriage bonds from 1760 to 1968 have been published.)

North Dakota. State Department of Health
Division of Vital Statistics
17th Floor, State Capitol
Bismarck, ND 58501

(Birth and death records date from 1883; marriages from July 1925. Earlier marriage records in custody of county judge in each county.)

Ohio. State Department of Health
Division of Vital Statistics
65 S. State Department Bldg.
Columbus, OH 43215

(Birth and death records date from 1908; marriage records from 1949. For earlier records write probate court in county where event occurred.)

Oklahoma. State Department of health
Division of Vital Statistics
3400 N. Eastern Avenue
Oklahoma City, OK 73105

(Birth and death records from 1908. Marriage records in courthouse of each county.)

Oregon. State Board of Health
Vital Statistics Section
P.O. Box 231
Portland, OR 27207

(Birth and death records from 1903; marriage records date from 1907. Marriage records dating from 1845 are in custody of clerk of county court.)

Pennsylvania. State Department of health
Division of Vital Statistics
P.O. Box 90
Harrisburg, PA 17120

(Birth and death records date from 1906. Records from 1852 to 1859 are in custody of register of wills in each county. Marriages before 1790 are published in Volume 2 of Pennsylvania Archives, Series 2.)

Rhode Island. State Department of Health
Division of Vital Statistics
Room 351
State Office Building
101 Smith Street
Providence, RI 02903

(Birth, death, and marriage records date from 1853. Earlier records are in town where event occurred. Records from 1636 have been published and arranged alphabetically by town where event occurred in the James N. Arnold Collection of Rhode Island Vital Records.)

South Carolina. State Board of Health
Bureau of Vital Statistics
J. Marion Sims Bldg.
Columbia, SC 29210

(Birth and death records date from 1915; marriage records from 1950. Charleston County Health Department records Charleston births from 1877 and deaths from 1821.)

Tennessee. State Department of Public Health
Division of Vital Statistics
Cordell Hull Building
Nashville, TN 37219

(Birth and death records from 1914. Nashville birth records date from 1881; Knoxville, 1881; Chattanooga, 1882. Death records: Nashville, 1872; Knoxville, 1887; Chattanooga, 1872. Marriage records before 1945 are in custody of county court clerk in each county.)

Texas. State Department of health
Bureau of Vital Statistics
410 E. 5th Street
Austin, TX 78701

(Birth and death records from 1903. Marriages before 1966 are in custody of county clerk of county where licenses were issued.)

Vermont. Office of Secretary of State
State House
Montpelier, VT 05602

(Birth and death records are in custody of town or city clerk where event occurred. Birth records from 1760; deaths from 1857, and marriages from 1780.)

Virgin Islands. Department of Health
Bureau of Vital Records
Charlotte Amalie, St. Thomas, VI 00802

(Birth and death records date from 1906; marriages from 1954. Marriage records are in the district court clerk's at St. Thomas.)

Virginia. State Department of Health
Bureau of Vital Records and Statistics
James Madison Bldg.
P.O. Box 1000
Richmond, VA 23208

(Birth and death records from 1912; marriages from 1853. Some birth records date from 1853 to 1896. The county clerk in each county has marriage records before 1853. Some cities had vital records before the state; Roanoke, 1891; Norfolk, 1892; Newport News, 1896; Portsmouth, 1900; Richmond, 1900; Lynchburg, 1910; Petersburg, 1900; and Elizabeth City County, 1900.)

Washington. State Department of Health
Bureau of Vital Statistics
Public Health Bldg.
Olympia, WA 98501

(Birth and death records date from 1907; marriages from 1968. Marriage records before 1968 are in custody of county auditor in each county as well as other earlier records.)

West Virginia. State Department of Health
Division of Vital Statistics
State Office Bldg. No. 3
Charleston, WV 25305

(Birth and death records date from 1917; marriages from 1921. Some records are in custody of county clerk in each county.)

Wisconsin. Division of Health
Bureau of Health Statistics
P.O. Box 309
Madison, WI 53701

(Birth and death records date from 1876; marriages from 1840. Some records go back to 1814. Marriage records are in custody of county clerk and of recorder of deeds in some counties.)

Wyoming. State Department of Health
Division of Vital Statistics
State Office Bldg.
Cheyenne, WY 82001

(Birth and death records date from 1909; marriages from 1914. Earlier marriage records are in custody of county clerk in each county.)

B. PUBLIC LIBRARIES

1. State Libraries and Archives

Alabama. Department of Archives and History
624 Washington Avenue
Montgomery, AL 36104

Alaska. Department of Education
Pouch G
State Capitol Bldg.
Juneau, AK 99801

Arkansas. Library Commission
506 1/2 Center Street
Little Rock, AR 72201

Arizona. Department of Administration
Division of Library Archives and Public Records
Phoenix, AZ 85007

Bahamas. Ministry of Education and Culture
Archives Section
PO Box N 3913
Nassau, New Providence, Bahamas

California. State Archives
1020 O Street
Sacramento, CA 98514

California. State Library
PO Box 2037
Sacramento, CA 95809

Canada. National Library
395 Wellington Street
Ottawa, Ontario, Canada

Colorado. State Library
1362 Lincoln Street
Denver, CO 80203

Connecticut. State Library
231 Capitol Avenue
Hartford, CT 06115

Delaware. Department of Historical and Cultural Affairs
Hall of Records
Dover, DE 19901

Delaware. Public Archives Commission
Hall of Records
Dover, DE 19901

England, London
The British Library
Reference Division
Great Russell Street
London

Florida. Division of Archives, History and Records Management
401 E. Gaines Street
Tallahassee, FL 32301

Florida. Division of Library Services
Department of State
Tallahassee, FL 32301

France. Archives Nationales
60 Rue des Frances-Bourgeois
Paris, France

Georgia. Department of Archives and History
330 Capitol Avenue
Atlanta, GA 30334

Georgia Division of Library Services
State Department of Education
156 Trinity Avenue, SW
Atlanta, GA 30303

Ghana. National Archives of Ghana
PO Box 3056
Accra, Ghana

Ghana. West African Historical Museum
PO Box 502
Cape Coast, Ghana

Guyana. National Library
PO Box 110
Georgetown, Guyana

Idaho. State Library
325 W. State Street
Boise, ID 83702

Illinois. State Archives
Archives Bldg.
Springfield, IL 62706

Illinois. State Historical Library
Old State Capitol
Springfield, IL 62706

Illinois. State Library
Centennial Memorial Building
Springfield, IL 62706

Indiana. Historical Bureau
State Library and Historical Building
Indianapolis, IN 46204

Indiana. State Library
140 N. Senate Avenue
Indianapolis, IN 46204

Iowa. State Department of History and Archives
E. 12th Street and Grand Avenue
Des Moines, IA 50319

Jamaica. Archives
Jamaica Library Service
Spanish Town PO Box 58
Kingston 5, Jamaica

Kansas. State Library
535 Kansas Avenue
Topeka, KS 66601

Kentucky. Department of Libraries
PO Box 537
Frankfort, KY 40601

Kenya. Cultural Centre
PO Box 40751
Harry Thuku Road
Nairobi, Kenya

Liberia. Government Public Library
Ashmun Street
Monrovia, Liberia

Louisiana. State Library
PO Box 131
Baton Rouge, LA 70800

Maine. State Archives
State House
Augusta, ME 04330

Maine. State Library
Augusta, ME 04330

Mali. Archives Nationales du Mali
Institut des Sciences Humaines
Koulouba
Bamako, Mali

Maryland. Division of Library Development and Services
State Department of Education
PO Box 8717
Baltimore, MD 21240

Michigan. State Library
735 E. Michigan Avenue
Lansing, MI 48913

Mississippi. Department of Archives and History
War Memorial Bldg.
PO Box 571
Jackson, MS 39205

Mississippi. Library Commission
405 State Office Bldg.
Jackson, MS 39201

Missouri. State Library
308 E. High Street
State Office Bldg.
Jefferson City, MO 65102

Montana. State Library
901 E. Lyndale Ave.
Helena, MT 59601

Nebraska. Public Library Commission
Lincoln, NB 68509

New Hampshire. State Library
20 Park Street
Concord, NH 03302

New Jersey. Bureau of Archives and History
State Library
185 W. State Street
Trenton, NJ 08625

New Mexico. State Library
300 Don Gaspar Street
Santa Fe, NM 87501

New York. Division of Library Development
New York State Library
State Department of Education
Albany, NY 12201

Nigeria. National Archives
PM B.4
University of Ibadan Post Office
Ibadan, Nigeria

Nigeria. National Library
4 Wesley Street
PMB 12626
Lagos, Nigeria

North Carolina. Department of Cultural Resources
Office of State Libraries
109 E. Jones St.
Raleigh, NC 27611

North Dakota. State Library Commission
Liberty Memorial Bldg.
Bismarck, ND 58501

Ohio. State Library
State Office Bldg.
Columbus, OH 43215

Oklahoma. Department of Libraries
200 18th Street, NE
Oklahoma City, OK 73105

Oregon. State Library
Salem, OR 97310

Pennsylvania. State Library
PO Box 1601
Walnut Street and Commonwealth Ave.
Harrisburg, PA 17126

Rhode Island. Department of State
Library Services
95 Davis Street
Providence, RI

South Carolina. Department of Archives
1430 Senate Street
Columbus, SC 29211

South Carolina. State Library
1500 Senate Street
PO Box 11469
Columbus, SC 29201

Sierra Leone. Public Archives
c/o Fourah Bay College Library
PO Box 87
Freetown, Sierra Leone, Africa

Tennessee State Library and Archives
403 7th Avenue
Nashville, TN 37219

Texas. Library and Historical Commission
1201 Brazos Street
PO Box 12927
Capitol Station
Austin, TX 78711

Texas. State Library
PO Box 12927
Capitol Station
Austin, TX 78711

Vermont. Department of Libraries
State of Vermont
Montpelier, VT 05601

Virgin Islands. Department of Libraries and Museums
PO Box 559
Government of the Virgin Islands
Charlotte Amalie, St. Thomas
Virgin Islands 00810

Virginia. State Library
12th and Capitol Streets
Richmond, VA 23219

Washington. State Library
Olympia, WA 98501

West Virginia. Library Commission
2004 Quarrier Street
Charleston, WV 25311

West Virginia. Department of Archives and History
400 E. Wing State Capitol
Charleston, WV 25305

Wisconsin. Division of Library Services
Wisconsin Hall
126 Langdon Street
Madison, WI 53703

Wyoming. State Archives and Historical Department
State Office Bldg.
Cheyenne, WY 82001

Wyoming. State Library
Supreme Court Bldg.
Cheyenne, WY 82001

2. Public Libraries Serving Predominantly Afro-American Communities

Libraries serving predominately black communities are a good source of genealogical information. Many of these libraries maintain significant collections of materials by and about Afro-Americans, receive Afro-American newspapers, and maintain clipping files. They also maintain files on local personalities, local speakers, and copies of printed programs of activities in the community. They may have special, local collections and memorabilia. In addition, these libraries hold basic information tools and offer interlibrary loan services.

The following list does not include all of the public libraries serving black communities, but it does include most of those that have declared "black studies, history, or culture" as focuses of their collections or are identified by the nature of the location of the library and its date of origin.

ALABAMA

Birmingham

East Ensley Branch
900-14th Street, Ensley
Birmingham, AL 35218

Georgia Road Branch Library
501 43rd Street, North
Birmingham, AL 35222
North Birmingham Branch Library
3200 North 27th Street
Birmingham, AL 35207

Smithfield Branch Library
One 8th Avenue West
Birmingham, AL 35204

Southside Branch Library
No. 2 Fifth Avenue, SW
Birmingham, AL 35211

Mobile

Toulminville Branch Library
2318 Stephens Road
Mobile, AL 36617

ARIZONA
Phoenix
Harmon Branch Library
411 Yavapai Street
Phoenix, AZ 85003

ARKANSAS
Little Rock
Study Center, East Little Rock Community Complex
2500 East 6th
Little Rock, AZ 72202

CALIFORNIA
Berkeley
South Berkeley Branch Library
1901 Russell Street
Berkeley, CA 97403

West Berkeley Branch Library
1125 University Avenue
Berkeley, CA 94702

Fresno
Fresno County Free Library
2420 Mariposa
Fresno, CA 93720

Long Beach
Burnett Branch Library
560 East Hill Street
Long Beach, CA 90806

Los Angeles
Angeles Mesa Branch
2700 West 52nd Street
Los Angeles, CA 90043

Exposition Park-Dr. Mary McCleod
Bethune Branch
3665 South Vermont Avenue
Los Angeles, CA 90007

Vermont Regional Branch Library
1201 West 48th Street
Los Angeles, CA 90037

Vernon Branch--Leon H. Washington Memorial Library
4504 South Central Avenue
Los Angeles, CA 90011

Watts Branch Library
1501 East 103rd St.
Los Angeles, CA 90002

Los Angeles County

A.C. Bilbrew Library
150 East El Segundo Blvd.
Los Angeles, CA 90061

Compton Library
240 West Compton Blvd.
Compton, CA 90220

Enterprise Library
2411 West Compton Blvd.
Compton, CA 90220

Florence Library
1610 East Florence Avenue
Los Angeles, CA 90001

Graham Library
1900 E. Firestone
Los Angeles, CA 90001

Holly Park Library
2150 West 120th Street
Hawthorne, CA 90250

Oakland

Melrose Branch Library
4805 Foothill Blvd.
Oakland, CA 94601

North Oakland Branch Library
3134 San Pablo Avenue
Oakland, CA 94608

West Oakland Branch Library
712 Peralta Street
Oakland, CA 94607

Sacramento
Del Paso Heights Library
920 Grand Avenue
Sacramento, CA 94838

Oak Park Branch Library
3301 5th Avenue
Sacramento, CA 98517

San Bernardino
Mary Belle Kellog Branch
1322 Muscott Street
San Bernardino, CA 92411

San Francisco
Anna E. Waden Branch Library
5075 3rd Street
San Francisco, CA 94124

Western Addition Branch
1550 Scott Street
San Francisco, CA 94115

Stockton
Fair Oaks Branch Library
2125 East Main Street
Stockton, CA 95202

COLORADO
Denver
Ford-Warren Library and Five Points Library
2825 High Street
Denver, CO 80205

Park Hill Library
Montview & Dexter
Denver, CO 80207

CONNECTICUT
Hartford
Albany Branch Library
1250 Albany Avenue
Hartford, CT 06112

Stamford
South End Branch Library
96 Broad Street
Stamford, CT 06901

DISTRICT OF COLUMBIA

Martin Luther King Memorial Library
901 G Street, N.W.
Washington, DC 20001

Anacostia Branch Library
Good Hope Road and 18th Street, S.E.
Washington, DC 20020

Langston Branch Library
701 24th Street, N.E.
Washington, DC 20002

Southeast Branch Library
7th and D Streets, S.E.
Washington, DC 20003

FLORIDA

Jacksonville

Eastside Branch Library
1390 Harrison Street
Jacksonville, FL 32206

Myrtle Avenue Branch
2304 North Myrtle Avenue
Jacksonville, FL 32209

St. Petersburg

James Weldon Johnson Branch Library
1035 3rd Avenue, South
St. Petersburg, FL 33705

GEORGIA

Atlanta

Collier Heights Branch Library
3571 Gordon Road, S.W.
Atlanta, GA 30331

Kirkwood Branch Library
250 Georgia Avenue
Atlanta, GA 30312

West Hunter Branch Library
1116 Hunter Street, S.W.
Atlanta, GA 30314

Columbus
Fourth Avenue Library
640 Fourth Avenue
Columbus, GA 31901

Savannah
Carnegie Branch Library
537 East Henry Street
Savannah, GA 31401

Yamacraw Branch Library
349 West Bryan Street
Savannah, GA 31401

ILLINOIS
Chicago
Auburn Branch Library
1364 West 79th Street
Chicago, IL 60620

Brainerd Branch Library
8945 South Loomis
Chicago, IL 60620

Carter G. Woodson Library-Community Library
9525 South Halstead Street
Chicago, IL 60628

Douglass Branch Library
3353 West 135th Street
Chicago, IL 60623

George C. Hall Branch Library
4801 South Michigan Avenue
Chicago, IL 60615

George W. Pullman Branch Library
11001 South Indiana
Chicago, IL 60643

Hamilton Park Library
7200 South Normal Blvd.
Chicago, IL 60621

Hiram Kelly Branch Library
6151 South Normal Blvd.
Chicago, IL 60621

Jefferey Manor Branch Library
2435 East 100th Street
Chicago, IL 60617

Legler Regional Branch Library
115 South Pulaski Road
Chicago, IL 60624

Near North Branch Library
451 West North Avenue
Chicago, IL 60610

Roosevelt Branch Library
1329 South Racine
Chicago, IL 60608

Sherman Park Branch Library
5440 South Racine
Chicago, IL 60617

Tulsey Park Sub-Branch Library
90th Street and St. Lawrence Avenue
Chicago, IL 60619

Whitney M. Young, Jr., Branch Library
7901 South Dr. Martin Luther King, Jr., Dr.
Chicago, IL 60619

Rockford
Montague Library Center
1238 South Winnebago Street
Rockford, IL 61102

INDIANA
Evansville
East Branch
340 E. Chandler Avenue
Evansville, IN

Indianapolis
Brightwood Branch Library
2435 North Sherman Drive
Indianapolis, IN 56218

IOWA
Des Moines
Mid City Library and Information Center
1305 University Avenue
Des Moines, IA 50314

KANSAS
Wichita
Wichita Public Library
223 South Main
Wichita, KS 67202

KENTUCKY
Louisville
Western Branch Library
604 South Tenth Street
Louisville, KY 40211

LOUISIANA
Baton Rouge
Carver Branch Library
1214 East Blvd.
Baton Rouge, LA 70802

Scotlandville Branch Library
1492 Harding Blvd.
Baton Rouge, LA 70807

MICHIGAN
Detroit
Duffield Branch
2507 West Grand Blvd.
Detroit, MI 48208

Parkman Branch Library
1766 Oakman Blvd.
Detroit, MI 48238

Flint
North Flint Branch Library
North Flint Shopping Plaza
West Pearson and Detroit Street
Flint, MI 48505

MINNESOTA
Minneapolis
Hosmer Community Hospital
347 East 36th Street
Minneapolis, MN 55408

Sumner Community Library
611 Emerson Avenue North
Minneapolis, MN 55411

MISSOURI
St. Louis
John Berry Meachum Branch Library
370 Grandel Square
St. Louis, MO 63108

Julia Davis Branch
4666 Natural Bridge Road
St. Louis, MO 63115

NEBRASKA
Omaha
Kellom Branch Library
221 Paul Street
Omaha, NB 68102

North Branch Library
29th and Ames
Omaha, NB 68111

NEVADA
Las Vegas
West Las Vegas Library
1402 North "D" Street
Las Vegas, NV 89106

NEW JERSEY
Jersey City
Claremont Branch Library
291 Martin Luther King Drive
Jersey City, NJ 07305

Newark
Clinton Branch Library
739 Bergen Street
Newark, NJ 07108

Springfield Branch Library
50 Hayes Street
Newark, NJ 07103

Weeguchic Branch Library
355 Osborne Terrace
Newark, NJ 07108

NEW YORK

Albany

Arbor Hill Branch Library
50 North Lark Street
Albany, NY 12208

John A. Howe Branch Library
Schuyler, Broad and Clinton Streets
Albany, NY 12202

Brooklyn

Bedford Branch Library
496 Franklin Avenue
Brooklyn, NY 11238

Brownsville Community Library
61 Glenmore Avenue
Brooklyn, NY 11212

Clinton Hill Branch Library
380 Washington Avenue
Brooklyn, NY 11238

Saratoga Community Library
8 Hopkinson Avenue
Brooklyn, NY 11233

Walt Whitman Community Library
93 St. Edwards Street
Brooklyn, NY 11205

Buffalo

Martin Luther King Branch Library
451 William Street
Towne Gardens Plaza
Buffalo, NY 14204

North Jefferson Street Branch
332 East Utica Street
Buffalo, NY 14208

New York

Countee Cullen Regional Branch Library
104 West 136th Street
New York, NY 10030

Macomb's Bridge Branch Library
2650 Seventh Avenue
New York, NY 10039

Tremont Branch Library
1866 Washington Avenue
Bronx, NY 10457

Washington Heights Branch Library
1000 St. Nicholas Avenue
New York, NY 10032

Rochester
Phillis Wheatley Community Library
13 Bronson Avenue
Rochester, NY 14608

NORTH CAROLINA
Charlotte
North Branch Library
2324 LaSalle Street
Charlotte, NC 28216

Greensboro
Southeast Branch Library
900 South Benbow Road
Greensboro, NC 27401

Raleigh
Richard B. Harrison Branch Library
1313 New Bern Avenue
Raleigh, NC 27610

OHIO
Cincinnati
Avondale Branch Library
3566 Reading Road
Cincinnati, OH 45229

Lincoln Park Branch Library
805 Lincoln Park Drive
Cincinnati, OH 45203

Madisonville Branch Library
4830 Whetsel Avenue
Cincinnati, OH 45227

Walnut Hills Branch Library
2533 Kemper Lane
Cincinnati, OH 45206

Cleveland

Arlington Branch Library
12332 Arlington Avenue
Cleveland, OH 44108

Collinwood Branch Library
856 West 152nd Street
Cleveland, OH 44110

East 131st Street Branch Library
3830 East 131st Street
Cleveland, OH 44103

Harvard-Lee Branch Library
4125 Lee Road
Cleveland, OH 44128

Langston Hughes Branch Library
2390 East 79th Street
Cleveland, OH 44104

Martin Luther King, Jr. Regional Branch Library
1962 East 107th Street
Cleveland, OH 44106

Miles Park Branch Library
Miles Park and East 93rd Street
Cleveland, OH 44105

Mount Pleasant Branch Library
14000 Kinsman Road
Cleveland, OH 44120

Sterling Branch Library
2200 East 30th Street
Cleveland, OH 44115

Superior Branch Library
1347 East 105th Street
Cleveland, OH 44106

Treasure House Branch Library
Crawford Road and East 86th Street
Cleveland, OH 44106

Union Branch Library
9319 Union Avenue
Cleveland, OH 44105

Woodlawn Branch Library
5806 Woodlawn Avenue
Cleveland, OH 44105

Columbus
Driving Park Branch Library
1566 East Livingston Avenue
Columbus, OH 43205

Martin Luther King Memorial Branch Library
1600 East Long Street
Columbus, OH 43203

Dayton
Madden Hills Branch Library
2542 Germantown Street
Dayton, OH 45429

Westwood Branch Library
320 Hoover Avenue
Dayton, OH 45407

Toledo
Kent Branch Library
3101 Collingwood Blvd.
Toledo, OH 43610

Mott Branch Library
1085 Don Street
Toledo, OH 43607

Youngstown
South Side Library
1711 Market Street
Youngstown, OH 44507

OKLAHOMA
Oklahoma City
Ralph Ellison Branch Library
2000 Northeast 23rd Street
Oklahoma City, OK 73160

OREGON
Portland
Albina Branch Library
3630 North Vancouver Avenue
Portland, OR 97227

North Portland Branch Library
512 North Killingsworth Avenue
Portland, OR 97217

PENNSYLVANIA
Pittsburgh
Homewood Branch Library
7101 Hamilton Avenue
Pittsburgh, PA 15208

Martin Luther King, Jr. Reading Center
Herron Avenue and Milwaukee Street
Pittsburgh, PA 15219

Wylie Avenue Branch Library
1909 Wylie Avenue
Pittsburgh, PA 15219

TENNESSEE
Chattanooga
South Chattanooga Branch Library
2500 South Market Street
Chattanooga, TN 37408

Knoxville
Burlington Branch Library
3615 McCalla Avenue
Knoxville, TN 37914

East Knoxville Branch Library
2301 McCalla Avenue
Knoxville, TN 37914

Memphis
Cherokee Branch Library
3300 Sharpe Avenue
Memphis, TN 38111

Levi Branch Library
3676 Highway 61 South
Memphis, TN 38109

North Branch Library
1192 Vollintine
Memphis, TN 38107

South Branch Library
185 East Norwood AVenue
Memphis, TN 38109

Vance Branch Library
531 Vance Avenue
Memphis, TN 38126

Nashville
Hadley Park Library
1039 28th Avenue North
Nashville, TN 37208

TEXAS
Austin
George Washington Carver Branch Library
1165 Angelina
Austin, TX 78702

Oak Springs Branch Library
2135 West Anderson Lane
Austin, TX 78757

Dallas
Lancaster-Kiest Branch Library
3039 South Lancaster
Dallas, TX 75216

Martin Luther King, Jr., Library/Learning Center
2922 Forest Avenue
Dallas, TX 75201

Houston
Dixon Branch Library
8002 Hirsch Road
Houston, TX 77016

Kashmere Gardens Branch
5411 Pardee
Houston, TX 77026

Lonnie E. Smith Branch Library
3624 Scott Street
Houston, TX 77004

VIRGINIA
Norfolk
Berkeley Branch Library
229 E. Berkeley Avenue
Norfolk, VA 23523

Blyden Branch Library
879 East Princess Anne Road
Norfolk, VA 23504

Brambleton Branch Library
1520 East Brambleton Avenue
Norfolk, VA 23504

Van Wyck Branch Library
345 West 15th Street
Norfolk, VA 23517

Portsmouth

Portsmouth Public Library
601 Court Street
Portsmouth, VA 23704

WASHINGTON

Seattle

Douglass-Truth Branch Library
23rd and East Yesler Way
Seattle, WA 98122

WISCONSIN

Milwaukee

Atkinson Neighborhood Library
1960 West Atkinson Avenue
Milwaukee, WI 53206

Center Street Neighborhood Library
2620 West Center Street
Milwaukee, WI 53206

Martin Luther King Neighborhood Library
310 East Locust Street
Milwaukee, WI 53202

C. SOME MAJOR COLLECTIONS AND LIBRARIES FOR GENEALOGY RESEARCH

Most libraries have resources that include genealogical information in one form or another. School, college, public and special libraries maintain basic biographical dictionaries and directories; periodicals, books, and miscellaneous sources that document people. Some libraries and special collections --community libraries, libraries of clubs and organizations-- collect materials and data that are organized and preserved for posterity and research purposes. This section lists some of the better-known libraries and collections that are more often cited and used in genealogical research.

The state archives in the traditional seventeen southern states have extremely valuable materials useful in Afro-American genealogy research. Unfortunately, most of these collections have not been indexed.

Amistad Research Center
400 Esplande Avenue
New Orleans, LA 70116

Relocated from Dillard University, New Orleans, Louisiana, the library's holdings include 20,000 book titles, 696 periodical subscriptions, 8,500,000 manuscripts, and 30,000 pamphlets. Materials focus on ethnic history and race relations with concentration on Afro-Americans, Native Americans, Chicanos, Asian Americans and Puerto Ricans. Much of the American Missionary Association collection that was at Fisk University has been relocated in this Center. Numerous collections of family papers, records of clubs and societies, and miscellaneous materials add to the usefulness of the Amistad Research Center.

Atlanta University Center
Robert W. Woodruff Library (Includes former
Trevor Arnett Collection)
Library Collection
111 Brawley Drive, NW
Atlanta, GA 30314

The Henry P. Slaughter Collection of this library contains 422 items, 1797-1890, of books, manuscripts, pamphlets, photographs, and other materials. Contents of the collection consist primarily of slave papers and correspondence of black leaders, abolitionists, and outstanding civil rights and political figures of the nineteenth century. Other noted collections include letters and papers of John Brown, Countee Cullen, C. Eric Lincoln, and others.

The Center for Research Libraries
5721 Cottage Grove Avenue
Chicago, IL 60637

The Center for Research Libraries is a non-profit organization operated for the purpose of increasing library materials available for research. Founded in 1949 by a group of ten universities, the Center now includes over 180 members and associate members and a collection of over three million volumes. The Center's holdings include microfilms of such collections as the American Missionary Association Archives, the Schomburg Collection, the Douglass Collection, *City Directories of the United States through 1881* and *State Census: An Annotated Bibliography of Population Censuses Taken after the Year 1790 by State and Territories of the United States*--all in microform.

Chicago Public Library

Carter G. Woodson Regional Library
The Vivian G. Harsh Collection of Afro-American History and Literature
9525 S. Halstead Street
Chicago, IL 60628

This collection covers all phases of Afro-American life from 1500 to the present. Includes over 11,000 monographs with particular strength in history, sociology, biography, and original manuscripts. Afro-American newspapers on microfilm date from 1927. Also papers on the American Missionary Association and vertical file of pamphlets and newspaper clippings.

Church of Jesus Christ Latter-Day Saints Library
Genealogical Department
50 East North Temple Street
Salt Lake City, UT 81450

Said to be the largest genealogical collection in the world, the LDS library in Salt Lake City houses research materials for the United States and Canada including American Indians and black ancestral materials. The U.S. section contains black genealogical information, including special censuses taken by the Southern states during the last century, and a beginning microfilm collection on records of blacks in Haiti and French Martinique. The Registry of Black Ancestry is a recent addition to services of this agency.

There are over 200 branches of the Library located throughout the United States. A complete list of the locations of the branches is available from the Salt Lake City main library. The LDS also has Branch Libraries through the United States and in many foreign countries.

The following is a list of branch libraries of the Genealogical Department of the Church of Jesus Christ Latter-Day Saints.

ALABAMA

Huntsville Branch, 106 Sanders Drive, SW, Huntsville 35802

ALASKA

Anchorage Branch, 2501 Maplewood St., Anchorage 99508
Fairbanks Branch, 1500 Cowles Street, Fairbanks 99701

ARKANSAS

Little Rock Branch, Highway 67, N., Jacksonville 72099

AUSTRALIA

Adelaide State Branch, 120 Gage St., Firle, South Australia
Melbourne Branch, 285 Heideberg Road, Northcote, Victoria, Australia
Sydney Branch, 55 Greenwich Road, Greenwich, Sydney, Australia
Sydney South Branch, Sutherland Ward Chapel, 196 Bath Road, Kirrawee, NSW, Australia

CALIFORNIA

Anaheim Branch, 440 North Loara (Rear) 92801
Bakersfield Branch, 1903 Bernard Street 93305
Barstow Branch, 2571 Barstow Road 92311
Cerritos Branch, 17909 Bloomfield 90701
Cerritos West Branch, 15311 South Pioneer Blvd., Norwalk 90650
Chico Branch, Stake Center, 1528 Esplanade 95926
Chovina Branch, 656 South Grand Avenue 91724
Eureka Branch, 2734 Dolbeer 95501
Fresno Branch, 1838 Echo Ave. N. 93704
Gridley Branch, 348 Spruce Street 95948
LaCrescento Branch, 4550 Raymond Avenue 91214
Long Beach East Branch, Stake Center, 1140 Ximeno Ave. 90804
Los Angeles Branch, 10741 Santa Monica Blvd. 90025
Los Angeles East Branch, 106 South Hillview Avenue 90022
Menlo Park Branch, Stake Center, 1105 Valparaiso Avenue 94025
Modesto Branch, 731 El Vista Avenue 95354
Monterey Branch, 1024 Noche Buena, Seaside 93940
Oakland Branch, 4780 Lincoln Avenue 94602
Redding Branch, 3410 Churn Creek Road 96002
Ridgecrest Branch, 501 Norma Street 93555
Riverside Branch, 5900 Grand Avenue 92504
Riverside West Branch, 4375 Jackson Street 92503
Sacramento Branch, 2745 Eastern Avenue 95821

San Bernardino Branch, 7000 Central Avenue 92408
San Diego Branch, 3705 10th Avenue 92103
San Jose Branch, 1336 Cherry Avenue 95125
San Luis Obispo Branch, 55 Casa Street 93401
Santa Barbara Branch, 478 Cambridge Drive, Goleta 93117
Santa Clara Branch, 875 Quince Avenue 95051
Santa Maria Branch, 1312 West Prune Avenue, Lompoc 93436
Santa Rosa Branch, 1725 Peterson Lane 95401
Stockton Branch, 814 Brookside Road 95207
Upland Branch, Stake Center, 785 North San Antonio 91786
Ventura Branch, 3501 Loma Vista Road 93003

CANADA
Calgary Alberta Branch, 2021 17th Avenue S.W.
Cardston Alberta Branch, 348 Third Street West
Edmondton Alberta Branch, 9010 85 Street
Hamilton Ontario Branch, Stake Center, 701 Stonechurch Road
Lethbridge Alberta Branch, Stake Center, 2410 28th Street S.
Toronto Ontario Branch, 95 Melbert Street, Etobicoke, Ontario
Vancouver B.C. Branch, Stake Center, 5280 Kincaid Street, Burnaby, Vancouver, British Columbia
Vernon B.C. Branch, Kelowna Ward, Glenmore and Ivans Street, Kelowna, British Columbia

COLORADO
Arvada Branch, 7080 Independence Street 80004
Boulder Branch, 4655 Table Mesa Drive 80303
Colorado Springs Branch, 20 North Cascade 80903
Denver Branch, Stake Center, 2710 South Monaco Parkway 80207
Denver North Branch, 100 East Malley Drive, Northglenn 80233
Durango Stake Branch, 1800 East Empire Street, Cortez 81301
Ft. Collins Branch, Stake Center, 600 East Swallow 80525
Grand Junction Branch, Stake Center, 543 Melody Lane 81501
LaJara Branch, Stake Center 81140
Littleton Branch, 1939 Easter Avenue 80120
Meeker Branch, 409 29th Street, Glenwood Springs 81641

CONNECTICUT
Hartford Branch, 30 Woodside Avenue, Manchester 06040

ENGLAND

Huddersfield Branch, Stake Center, 12 Halifax Road, Birchencliffe
Sunderland Branch, Stake Center, Alexandra Road, Sunderland, Tyne and Wear, England

FLORIDA

Jacksonville Branch, 4087 Hendricks Avenue 32207
Miami Branch, 1350 North West 95th Street 33147
Orlando Branch, 45 East Par Avenue 32804
Pensacola Branch, 5673 North 9th Avenue 33567
Tampa Branch, 4106 Fletcher Avenue 33612

GEORGIA

Macon Branch, 3006 14th Avenue, Columbus 31904
Sandy Springs Branch, 1155 Mt. Vernon Highway, Dunwoody 30338

HAWAII

Honolulu West Branch, Stake Center, 1733 Beckley St. 96819
Kaneohe Branch, 46-117 Halaulani Street 96863
Laie Branch BYU, Hawaii Library 96762

IDAHO

Bear Lake Branch, Bear Lake County Library, 138 North 6th Street, Montpelier 83254
Blackfoot West Branch, Stake Center, 6 miles northwest of Blackfoot on Pioneer Road 83221
Boise Branch, 325 West State Street 83702
Burley Branch, 224 East 14th Street 83318
Driggs Branch, Stake Center, 221 North 1st E. 83422
Idaho Falls Branch, 290 Chestnut Street 83402
Iona Branch, Stake Center, Iona Road and Ririe, Hwy. 26, Idaho Falls 83401
Lewiston Branch, Stake Center, 9th and Preston 83501
Malad Branch, 400 North 200 West 83252 (Malad City)
Moore Branch, Lost River Stake Center 83255
Pocatello Branch, 156 1/2 South 6th Avenue 83201
Salmon Branch, Salmon River Stake Center 83467
Twin Falls Branch, Maurice Street N. 83301
Upper Snake River Branch, Ricks College Library, Rexburg 83440

ILLINOIS

Champaign Branch, 604 West Windsor Road 61820
Chicago Heights Branch, 402 Longwood Drive 60411
Naperville Branch, 25 West 341 Chicago Avenue 60540
Wilmette Branch, 2801 Lake Avenue 60091

INDIANA
Ft. Wayne Branch, 5401 St. Joe Road 46815
Indianapolis Branch, Stake Center, 900 E. Stop 11 Rd. 46227

IOWA
Des Moines Branch, 3301 Ashworth Road, West Des Moines 50265

KANSAS
Wichita Branch, 7011 13th Street 67206

KENTUCKY
Louisville Branch, 1000 Hurstborne Lane 40222

LOUISIANA
Baton Rouge Branch, 5686 Winbourne Avenue 70805

MAINE
Augusta Branch, Hasson Street, Farmingdale 04330

MARYLAND
Silver Spring Branch, 500 Randolph Road 20904

MASSACHUSETTS
Boston Branch, Brown St. and South Ave., Weston 02193

MEXICO
Colonia Juarez Branch, Colonia Juarez, Chihuahua, Mexico
Mexico City Branch, Churu Busco Stake Center, Mexico City, Mexico

MICHIGAN
Bloomfield Hills Branch, 425 North Woodward Avenue 48013
Dearborn Branch, 20201 Rotunda Drive 48124
Lansing Branch, Stake Center, 431 East Saginaw St., East Lansing 48906
Midland Branch, 1700 West Sugnut Road 48640

MINNESOTA
Minneapolis Branch, 2801 Douglas Drive, N. 55422

MISSOURI
Columbia Branch, Highway 63, S. 65202
Kansas City Branch, 8144 Holmes St. 64131
St. Louis Branch, 10445 Clayton Road, Frontenac 63131
Springfield Branch, 1322 South Campbell 65807

MISSISSIPPI
Hattiesburg Branch, Stake Center, U.S. 11, S. 39401

MONTANA
Billings Branch, 1711 6th Street, E. 59801
Butte Branch, Dillon Chapel, 715 E. Bannock St. 59701
Great Falls Branch, 1401 9th Street, N.W. 59404
Helena Branch, 1610 East 6th Avenue 59601
Kalispell Branch, Buffalo Hill 59901
Missoula Branch, 3201 Bancroft Street 59801

NEBRASKA
Omaha Branch, 11027 Martha Street 68144

NEVADA
Ely Branch, Avenue E and 9th Street 89301
Fallon Branch, 750 West Richards Street 89406
Las Vegas Branch, 509 South 9th Street 89101
Reno Branch, Washoe Public Library, 310 South Center St. 89501

NEW JERSEY
Morristown Branch, 140 White Oak Ridge road, Summit 07960
East Brunswick Branch, 303 Dunhams's Corner road 08816

NEW MEXICO
Albuquerque Branch, 5709 Haines Avenue, N.E. 87110
Farmington Branch, 400 West Apache 87401

NEW YORK
Albany Branch, 411 Loudon Road, Loudonville 12211
Buffalo Branch, 1424 Maple Road 14221
Ithaca Branch, 305 Murray Hill Road, Vestal 14850
New York Branch, 2 Lincoln Square (3d Floor), Broadway at 65th Street 10023
Plainview Branch, 160 Washington Avenue 11803
Rochester Branch, 460 Kreag Road, Fairport 14450

NEW ZEALAND
Auckland Branch, No. 2 Scotia Place, Auckland CI
Canterbury Branch, 25 Fendalton Road, Christchurch
Temple View Branch, Temple View, New Zealand
Wellington Branch, Wellington Chapel, 140 Moxham Avenue

NORTH CAROLINA
Charlotte Branch, 3020 Hilliard Drive 28205
Raleigh Branch, 5100 Six Forks Road 27609

OHIO

Cincinatti Branch, 5505 Bosworth Place 45212
Cleveland Branch, 25000 Westwood Road, Westlake 44145
Columbus Branch, 3646 Lieb Street 43214
Dayton Branch, 1500 Shiloh Springs Road 45426

OKLAHOMA

Oklahoma City Branch, 5020 Northwest 63d 73132
Tulsa Branch, 12110 East 7th Street 74128

OREGON

Beaverton Branch, 10425 Southwest Beaverton, Hillsdale Highway 97005
Bend Branch, Stake Center, 1260 Thompson Drive 97701
Coos Bay Branch, 3950 Sherman Avenue, North Bend 97420
Corvalis Branch, 4141 Northwest Harrison Blvd. 97330
Eugene Branch, 3550 West 18th Street 97402
Gresham Branch, 3500 Southeast 182d 97030
LaGrande Branch, Old Welfare Bldg., 2504 N. Fir 97850
Medford Branch, 2980 Juanipero Way 97504
Nyssa Branch, West Alberta Avenue 97913
Portland Branch, 2931 Northeast Harrison S.E. = 97214
Portland East Branch, 2215 Northeast 106th 97220
Salem Branch, 4550 Lone Oak, S.E. 97302

PENNSYLVANIA

Gettysburg Branch, 2100 Hollywood Drive, York 17325
Philadelphia Branch, 721 Paxon Hollow Road, 19008 Broomall
State College Branch, Whitehall Road, State College 16801

SOUTH AFRICA

Johannesburg Branch, 1 Hunter St., Highlands

SOUTH CAROLINA

Columbia Branch, 4440 Ft. Jackson Blvd. 29209

TENNESSEE

Knoxville Branch, 400 Kendall road 37919
Memphis Branch, 4520 Winchester Road 38118
Tennessee South Branch, Old Shelbyville Hwy., Tullahoma 37388

TEXAS

Austin Branch, 2111 Parker Lane 78741
Beaumont Branch, Williamson Ward Chapel, Vidor 77662
Corpus Christi Branch, 505 North Mesquite St. 78401

Dallas Branch, 616 West Keist Blvd. 75216
Dallas North Branch, 10701 Lake Highlands Drive 75218
El Paso Branch, 3651 Douglas Avenue 79903
Ft. Worth Branch, Stake Center, 4401 Northeast Loop 820, North Richland Hills 76148
Houston Branch, 1101 Bering Drive 77057
Houston East Branch, Stake Center, 3000 Broadway 77017
Longview Branch, 1700 Blueridge Parkway 75605
Odessa Branch, 2011 Washington 77503
San Antonio Beach, 2103 St. Cloud Rd. 78228

UTAH
Beaver Branch, 15 North, 100 West 84713
Brigham City South Branch, 865 South 3d W 84302
Cache Branch, 950 North Main, Logan 84321
Cedar City Branch, 256 South, 900 West 84720
Duchesne Branch, Stake Center, Duchesne 84021
Fillmore Branch, Stake Center, 21 South, 300 West
Kanab Branch, Stake Center 84631
Monticello Branch, 225 East 2d, N., Blanding 84535
Mt. Pleasant Branch, Mt. Pleasant Stake Center 84647
Ogden Branch, 339 21st Street 84401
Price Branch, 85 East Fourth, N. 84501
Richfield Branch, 91 South 2d, W. 84701
Roosevelt Branch, 447 East Lagoon Street 84066
St. George Branch, 401 South, 400 East 84770
Santaquin Branch, Stake Center 84655
South Jordan Branch, 2450 West, 10400 South
Springville Branch, 245 South, 600 East 84663
Uintah Basin Branch, 613 West 2d, S., Vernal 84078
Utah Valley Branch, 405 HBL Library, BYU, Provo 84601

VIRGINIA
Annandale Branch, 3900 Howard Street 22003
Norfolk Branch, 4760 Princess Anne road, Virginia Beach 23502
Oakton Branch, Hunter Mill Road 22124
Richmond Stake Branch, 5600 Monument Avenue 23226

WALES
Merthyr Tydfil Branch, Top of Nantygwenith St. Georgetown, Merthyr, Tydfil, Wales

WASHINGTON
Bellevue Branch, 10675 Northeast 20th Street 98004
Everett Branch, Everett Stake Center 98201
Longview Branch, 1721 30th Avenue 98632
Moses Lake Branch, 1515 Division 98837

Mt. Vernon Branch, 1700 Hazel 98273
Olympia Branch, Olympia Stake Center 98501
Pasco Branch, Stake Center, 2004 N. 24th St. 99301
Quincy Branch, 1101 2d, S.E. 98848
Richland Branch, 1720 Thayer Drive 99352
Seattle North Branch, 5701 8th, N.E. 98105
Spokane Branch, North 919 Pines Road 99206
Tacoma Branch, South 12th and Pearl Streets 98465
Vancouver Branch, Stake Center, 10509 S.E. 5th Street 98664
Yakima Branch, 705 South 38th Avenue 98902

WISCONSIN
Appleton Branch, Lodge Hall, Main Street, Shawano 54166
Milwaukee Branch, 9600 West Grange Avenue, Hales Corner 53130

WYOMING
Afton Branch, 347 Jefferson Avenue 83110
Casper Branch, 700 South Missouri 82609
Cheyenne Branch, 2800 Central Avenue 82001
Cody Branch, Cody Ward Chapel 82414
Evanston Branch, 1224 Morse Lee St. 82930
Lovell Branch, 50 West Main 82431

Duke University
William R. Perkins Library
Manuscript Division
Durham, NC 27706

Materials in the manuscript collection date from 1500 and include 7,000,000 items with more than 6,700 collections of correspondences, scrapbooks, diaries, account books, and plantation records. Papers, letters, and documents of private families include business transactions (purchase and sale of slaves), records of overseers (work and ration books), physicians' account books, and other original materials from all over the south.

Filson Club
118 West Breckenridge Street
Louisville, KY 40203

The Filson Club is a "privately endowed and supported historical society working actively to aid historical research, education, and publication." The library of the Club is noted for its genealogical holdings that include family genealogies, abstracts of wills, deeds, marriages, and court records; manuscripts covering the period from pioneer days to the present, minute books, muster rolls, diaries, and notable materials on the Shaker Colony at Pleasant Hill in Mercer County. Census returns for Kentucky and a large collection of Kentucky newspapers, maps, prints, and pictures are also included in the collection. The superior collection of family papers and manuscripts includes bills of sale for slaves, records of fugitive slaves, inventories of estates, manumission records and letters about specifically named slaves. The library also has numerous records for adjoining states, particularly Virginia, Maryland and Pennsylvania.

Fisk University, Library and Media Center
7th Avenue North
Nashville, TN 37203

The Fisk University collection includes materials on aspects of the Negro in America, Africa, and the Caribbean. Antislavery papers and documents of slavery such as bills of sale, manumission papers and related materials are included in this collection. The American Missionary Association papers were long a central focus of this collection; much of this collection has since been removed to the Amistad Center in New Orleans, Louisiana. Manuscripts in the collection include papers of such personalities as Scott Joplin, Langston Hughes, James Weldon Johnson, and W. C. Handy.

Howard University
Founders Library
Moorland-Spingarn Research Center
2400 6th Street, NW
Washington, DC 20059

Established in 1914, the collection covers Africa, Afro-Americans, the Caribbean, and South America. Thousands of photographs, numerous vertical files, and the 120 processed manuscript and archival collections are valuable sources for genealogical study.

Library of Congress
Washington, DC

The Library of Congress through its Local History and Genealogy Room maintains 30,000 published family histories indexed by surname and 90,000 works on local history. The Library also has a number of plantation records, family accounts, and diaries of the Old South. Some manumission records and other records of the antebellum south are also included. A complete list of the Library's genealogical holdings is found in the *Guide to Genealogical Holdings at the Library of Congress* and the *Guide to Local History at the Library of Congress*.

Louisiana State University
Department of Archives
Baton Rouge, LA 70803

Louisiana State University has a wealth of family papers of former slaveholders, church records that show slave and free black members, business records, slave inventories arranged in family groups or listings of the mother's name with the names and birth dates of her children, and papers of free black families of the Civil War period.

National Archives and Record Service
United States General Services Administration
Washington National Records Center
Washington, DC 20409

The National Archives has the largest government collection of primary source materials for genealogy research. The records and materials include record groups having related information on the United States District Courts, the Select Committee on Slavery and the Treatment of Freedmen, the Bureau of Colored Troops and Slave Claims Commission; schedules of the federal census of population, military service records and pension claims, plantation records, and bills of sale slave records including ships manifests, lists of free black heads of household in the 1790 census, and miscellaneous materials and records.

Federal Archives and Records Centers are located in regions throughout the country. Most of the centers have extensive microfilm holdings of Federal Census Schedules for that region, in addition to regional materials. A listing of each center's holdings may be obtained by writing the center or by telephone.

Federal Archives and Records Centers

Atlanta Center
1557 St. Joseph Avenue
East Point, GA 30344

This center serves Alabama, Florida, Georgia, Kentucky, Mississippi, North Carolina, South Carolina, and Tennessee.

Boston Center
380 Trapelo Road
Waltham, MA 02154

Serves Connecticut, Maine, Massachusetts, New Hampshire, Rhode Island, and Vermont.

Chicago Center
7358 South Pulaski Road
Chicago, IL 60629

Serves Illinois, Indiana, Michigan, Minnesota, Ohio, and Wisconsin.

Denver Center
Building 48
Denver Federal Center
Denver, CO 80225

Serves Colorado, Montana, North Dakota, Utah, and Wyoming.

Fort Worth Center
4900 Hemphill Street
P.O. Box 6216
Fort Worth, TX 76115

Serves Arkansas, Louisiana, New Mexico, Oklahoma, and Texas.

Kansas City Federal Archives and Records Center
2306 East Bannister Road
Kansas City, MO 64131

Records for Iowa, Kansas, Missouri, and Nebraska.

Los Angeles Federal Archives and Records Center
24000 Avila Road
Laguna Niguel, CA 92677

Records for Arizona, Southern California, and Clark County, Nevada.

New York Federal Archives and Records Center
Building 22-MOT Bayonne
Bayonne, NJ 07002

Records for New Jersey, New York, Puerto Rico, and the Virgin Islands.

Philadelphia Federal Archives and Records Center
5000 Wissahickon Avenue
Philadelphia, PA

Records for Delaware, Pennsylvania, District of Columbia, Maryland, Virginia, and West Virginia.

San Francisco Federal Archives and Records Center
1000 Commodore Drive
San Bruno, CA 94066

Records for Northern California, Hawaii, Nevada (except Clark County), and territories in the Pacific. Includes special materials pertaining to American Samoa.

National Genealogical Society Library
1921 Sunderland Place, NW
Washington, DC 20036

The National Genealogical Society was established in 1903 to promote interest in and scholarly research in genealogy. Its library includes published and unpublished materials in genealogy, local history and heraldry, and family histories. The Society publishes the *National Genealogical Society Quarterly* that has reprinted family histories and an invaluable alphabetical *Index to Revolutionary War Pensioners*. The library is open to the public for a fee.

National Society of the Daughters of the American Revolution.
1776-D Street, NW
Washington, DC 20006

This library has over 70,000 volumes of print, and tens of thousands of local history records. Copies of local records made by members of chapters throughout the country as well as published works are included in the collection. Other records include abstracts of Revolutionary war pensions, federal pension schedules, members' genealogies, mortality schedules, and an index to patriots. The library is open to the public for a fee except during the month of April.

New York Public Library
Schomburg Center for Research in Black Culture
103 West 135th Street
New York, NY 10030

This library is second only to the National Archives in the body of information useful to the Afro-American family historian. The Center's collection includes a complete set of federal population censuses from 1790-1890, manu-- scripts, pictures and memorabilia, Afro-American family histories, specialized histories, a half century of black periodicals, and the Harry A. Williamson Collection of Negro Masonry. The Center accepts family histories of those Afro-Americans who submit them.

D. HISTORICALLY BLACK COLLEGES AND UNIVERSITIES

Libraries, archives, and special collections at such black institutions as Fisk and Howard Universities are generally acknowledged as agencies with general and specific resources for Afro-American genealogy. Other colleges and universities may not think of the library and other campus resources as having meaningful materials for genealogy research, but, in fact, all institutions of higher learning have resources that are of significant value in Afro-American genealogy research. Student and alumni records; records of admission, records and momentos of campus organizations and activities, campus publications, programs of convocations and commencements, employment applications, and personnel files can be found on *all* campuses and provide date on individuals.

Alcorn State University Library
Alcorn State
Lorman, MI 39096

Will W. Alexander Library
Dillard University
2601 Gentilly Boulevard
New Orleans, LA 70122

Alumni Library
Knoxville College
Knoxville, TN 37921

Trevor Arnett Library
(Refer to Robert W. Woodruff Library)
Atlanta University
273 Chestnut St., SW
Atlanta, GA 30314

W.R. Banks Library
Prairie View A. & M. University
Prairie View, TX 77445

Blazer Library
Kentucky State College
Frankfort, KY 40601

F.D. Bluford Library
North Carolina A&T State University
Greensboro, NC 27411

Hallie A. Brown Memorial Library
Central State University
Wilberforce, OH 45384

Brown-Daniels Library
Tennessee State University
Centennial Blvd.
Nashville, TN 37203

Warren A. Candler
Paine College
Augusta, GA 30901

Andrew Carnegie Library
Livingstone College
Salisbury, NC 28144

Carnegie Library
Wilberforce University
Wilberforce, OH 45384

Charles W. Chesnutt Library
Fayetteville State University
Fayetteville, NC 28301]

William J. Clark Library
Virginia Union University
Richmond, VA 23220

Thomas Winston Cole, Sr., Library
Wiley College
Marshall, TX 75670

Samuel H. Coleman Library
Florida A&M University
P.O. Box 78-A Florida A&M
Tallahassee, FL 32307

L. Zenobia Coleman Library
Tougaloo College
Tougaloo, MI 39174

J.K. Daniels Library
Lane College
545 Lane Avenue
Jackson, TN 38301

University of the District of Columbia
Library/Media Services
425 2nd Street, N.W.
Washington, DC 20001

Frederick Douglass Library
University of Maryland Eastern Shore
Princess Anne, MD 21853

Drain-Jordan Library
West Virginia State College
Institute, W. VA 25112

J.F. Drake Memorial Learning Resources Center
Alabama A&M University
Huntsville, AL 35762

James B. Duke Memorial Library
Johnson C. Smith University
100 Beatties Ford Road
Charlotte, NC 28216

Fisk University Library Media Center
17th & Jackson Streets
Nashville, TN 37203

J.S. Flipper Library
Allen University
Columbia, SC 29204

Hollis B. Frissel Library
Tuskegee Institute
Tuskegee, AL 36088

The D.R. Glass Library
Texas College
2404 N. Grand Avenue
Tyler, TX 75701

Asa H. Gordon Library
Savannah State College
Savannah, GA 31404

Marquis L. Harris Library
Clark College
240 Chestnut Street, S.W.
Atlanta, GA 30314

M.L. Harris Library
Philander Smith College
Little Rock, AR

G. Lamar Harrison Library
Langston University
Langston, OK 73050

Margaret Rood Hazard Library
Albany State College
Albany, GA 31705

Hogan-Steward Learning Resources Center
Southwestern Christian College
Box 10
Terrell, TX 75160

Thomas F. Holgate Library
Bennett College
Greensboro, NC 27420

Howard University Libraries
Howard University
500 Howard Place, NW
Washington, DC 20059

Langston Hughes Memorial Library
Lincoln University
Lincoln University, PA 19352

Henry Alexander Hunt Library
Fort Valley State College
Fort Valley, GA 31030

William C. Jason Library-Learning Center
Delaware State College
Dover, DE 19901

Johnston Memorial Library
Virginia State College
Petersburg, VA 23803

Jordan-Thomas Library
Morris Brown College
643 Martin Luther King Blvd.
Atlanta, GA 30314

S.S. Kresge Learning Resources
Meharry Medical College
Nashville, TN 37208

A.C. Lewis Memorial Library
Grambling State University
Grambling, LA 71245

G.R. Little Library
Elizabeth City State University
1001 Parkview Drive
Elizabeth City, NC 27909

H.V. Manning Library
Claflin College
Orangeburg, SC 29115

Thurgood Marshall Library
Bowie State College
Bowie, MD 20715

Parlett Moore Library
Coppin State College
2500 West North Avenue
Baltimore, MD 21216

Morgan State University Library
Cold Spring Lane and Hillen Road
Baltimore, MD 21239

Morristown College Library
Morristown, TN 37814

C.G. O'Kelly LIbrary
Winston-Salem State University
Winston-Salem, NC 27102

Olin Library
Jarvis Christian College
Drawer G
Hawkins, TX 75765

Inman E. Page Library
Lincoln University
Jefferson City, MO 65101

Daniel Payne College Library
201 W. Sayreton Rd.
Birmingham, AL 35214

Leslie Pinckney Hill Library
Cheyney State College
Cheyney, PA 19352
I.D. Pinson Memorial Library
Morris College
North Main Street
Sumter, SC 29150

Hollis F. Price Library
LeMoyne-Owens College
807 Walker Avenue
Memphis, TN 38126

Leontyne Price Library
Rust College
Holly Springs, MS 38635

Sage Memorial Library
Barber Scotia College
145 Cabarrus Avenue
Concord, NC 28025

Saint Augustine College Library
Saint Augustine College
Oakwood Avenue
Raleigh, NC 27611

St. Phillips College Library
2111 Nevada St.
San Antonio, TX 78203

Henry T. Sampson Library
Jackson State University
1325 J.R. Lynch Street
Jackson, MS 39217

Savery Library
Talladega College
Talladega, AL 35160

Shaw University
Learning Resources Center
118 East South Street
Raleigh, NC 27602

James E. Shepard Memorial Library
North Carolina Central University
Durham, NC 27707

William H. Sheppard Library
Stillman College
3600 15th Street
Tuscaloosa, AL 35401

Southern University Library
Baton Rouge, LA 70813

Southern University in New Orleans Library
6400 Press Drive
New Orleans, LA 70126

Texas Southern University Library
Texas Southern University
3201 Wheeler
Houston, TX 77004

H.V. Tookes Library
Edward Waters College
1658 Kings Road
Jacksonville, FL 32209

Voorhees College Library
Voorhees College
Denmark, SC 29042

John Brown Watson, Library
University of Arkansas at Pine Bluff
Pine Bluff, AR 71601

James Herbert White Library
Mississippi Valley State University
Itta Bena, MO 38941

Miller F. Whittaker Library
South Carolina State College
P.O. Box 1991
Orangeburg, SC 29117

Xavier University Library
7325 Palmetto and Pine St.
New Orleans, LA 70124

The Zale Library
Bishop College
3837 Simpson-Stuart Road
Dallas, TX 75241

E. SOME GENEALOGICAL AND HISTORICAL SOCIETIES AND ORGANIZATIONS

Many genealogical and historical societies and organizations maintain libraries and specialized collections. Resources of these agencies and groups are often useful to the Afro-American genealogy researcher. Some of the organizations with well-known research collections such as the Filson Club of Louisville, Kentucky are discussed under "Research Libraries and Collections," in this section. Names and addresses of some other groups whose collections and libraries are likely to hold significant materials useful in Afro-American genealogy research are included in the following listing. An increasing number of Afro-American genealogical and historical societies have been organized in recent years, and some of these groups have been added to the listing and noted with an asterisk (*).

For a complete listing of genealogical societies in America Consult Mary Kay Meyer's *Directory of Genealogical Societies of the United States*. The *Directory of Historical Societies and Agencies in the United States and Canada*, published by the American Association for State and Local History gives the names and addresses of specialized historical societies for racial, religious, and ethnic groups.

*African-American Family History Association
2077 Bent Way Creek, SW
Atlanta, GA 30301

Afro-American Cultural and Historical Society/
Historical Museum
8716 Harkness Rd.
Cleveland, OH 44106

Afro-American Genealogical and Historical
Society of Chicago
7933 S. Michigan
Chicago, IL 60619

*Afro-American Historical and Genealogical
Society, Inc.
PO Box 13086 T Street Station
Washington, DC 20009

*Afro-American Historical Association of the
Niagra Frontier
332 E. Utica
Buffalo, NY 14208

Alabama Historical Association
3121 Carlisle Rd.
Birmingham, AL 35213

Arizona Historical Society
949 E. 2nd Street
Tucson, AZ 85719

Ark-La-Tex Genealogical Association
PO Box 4462
Shreveport, LA 71104

*Association for the Study of Afro-American
Life and History
1538 9th Street, NW
Washington, DC 20009

Atlanta Historical Society, Inc.
3099 Andrews Drive, NW
Atlanta, GA 30305

California Historical Society
2090 Jackson Street
San Francisco, CA 94115

*Connecticut Afro-American Historical Society, Inc.
444 Orchard Street
New Haven, CT 06511

Connecticut Historical Society
1 Elizabeth Street
Hartford, CT 06105

Daughters of the American Revolution,
National Society
1776 D Street, NW
Washington, DC 20006

Delaware, Historical Society of
505 Market Street
Wilmington, DE 19801

*DuSable Museum of African-American History
3806 S, Michigan Avenue
Chicago, IL 60653

Georgia Historical Society
501 Whitaker Street
Savannah, GA 31401
Illinois State Historical Society
Old State Capitol
Springfield, IL 62706

Indiana Historical Society
140 N. Senate Ave.
Indianapolis, IN 46204

Kentucky Historical Society
PO Box H
Frankfort, KY 40601

*Kenya, Historical Association of
PO Box 30710
Nairobi, Kenya

Louisiana Historical Association
PO Box 44422
Capitol Station
Baton Rouge, LA 70804

Louisiana Historical Society
630 Maison Blanche Bldg.
921 Canal Street
New Orleans, LA 70112

Maine Historical Society
485 Congress Street
Portland, ME 04111

Maryland Historical Society
201 W. Monument Street
Baltimore, MD 21201

Massachusetts Historical Society
1154 Boyleston Street
Boston, MA 02215

Michigan, Historical Society of
2117 Washtenaw Avenue
Ann Arbor, MI 48104

Minnesota Historical Society
690 Cedar Street
St. Paul, MN 55101

Mississippi Historical Society
PO Box 571
Jackson, MS
Missouri Historical Society
Jefferson Memorial Bldg.
St. Louis, MO 63112

Montana Historical Society
Jefferson Memorial Bldg.
St. Louis, MO 63112

Montana Historical Society
225 N. Robert Street
Helena, MT 59601

National Genealogical Society
1921 Sunderland Place, NW
Washington, DC 20036

Native New Yorkers Historical Association
503 W. 22nd Street
New York, NY 10011

Nebraska State Historical Society
1500 R Street
Lincoln, NB 68508

New England Historic Genealogical Society
101 Newbury Street
Boston, MA 02116

New Hampshire Historical Society
30 Park Street
Concord, NH 03301

New London County Historical Society
Shaw Mansion
11 Blinman Street
New London, CT 06320

New Mexico, Historical Society of
PO Box 1442
Socorro, NM 87801

New York Genealogical and Biographical Society
122 E. 58th Street
New York, NY 10022

New York State Historical Association
PO Box 391
Cooperstown, NY 13326

Newport Historical Society Library
82 Touro Street
Newport, RI 02840

*Nigeria, Historical Society of
c/o Department of History
University of Ife
Ile-Ife, Nigeria

North Dakota, State Historical Society of
Liberty Memorial Building
Bismarck, ND 58501

Ohio Historical Society
Ohio Center
Columbus, OH 43211

Oklahoma Historical Society
Historical Bldg.
Oklahoma City, OK 73105

Oregon Historical Society
1230 W. Park Avenue
Portland, OR 97205

Pennsylvania, Genealogical Society of
1300 Locust Street
Philadelphia, PA 19107

Pennsylvania, Historical Society of
1300 Locust Street
Philadelphia, PA 19107

*Perkins, Matilda Delaney International, Inc.
Educational, Historical, and Preservation Association
PO Box 6403
Shreveport, LA 71106

*Rhode Island Black Heritage Society
45 Hamilton Street
Providence, RI 02907

Rhode Island Historical Society
52 Power Street
Providence, RI 02906

St. Augustine Historical Society
271 Charlotte Street
St. Augustine, FL 32084
Society of Genealogist
37 Harrington Gardens
SW 74JX
London, England

South Carolina Historical Society
Chalmers and Meeting Streets
Charleston, SC 29401

South Dakota State Historical Society
Soldiers' and Sailors' Memorial Bldg.
Pierre, SD 57501

Southern Florida, Historical Society of
3290 S. Miami Avenue
Miami, FL 33129

*Tarrant County Black Historical
and Genealogical Society
1150 E. Rosedale
Fort Worth, TX

Tennessee Historical Society
200 State Library and Archives Bldg.
Nashville, TN 37219

Texas Historical Association
Richardson Hall 2/306
University Station
Austin, TX 78712

Vermont Historical Society
Pavilion Bldg.
Montpelier, VT 05602

Virginia Historical Society
428 N. Boulevard
Richmond, VA 23221
Washington State Historical Society
315 N. Stadium Way
Tacoma, WA 98403

West Virginia Historical Society
400 E. Wing, State Capitol
Charleston, WV 25305

*Western Pennsylvania Research
and Historical Society, Inc.
1810 Funston Street
Pittsburgh, PA 15325

Western Reserve Historical Society
10825 E. Boulevard
Cleveland, OH 44106

*Williams, Fred Hart Genealogical Society
Detroit Public Library
Detroit, MI 48208

Wilson, Mariam B. Foundation
Old Slave Mart Museum
6 Chalmers Street
Charleston, SC 29401

Wisconsin, State Historical Society of
816 State Street
Madison, WI 53706

Witchita Historical Museum Association
537 E. Douglas
Witchita, KS 67218

KEY TO LOCATION SYMBOLS

AlA&ML	Alabama Agricultural and Mechanical State University Library, Huntsville.
AlDAR	Alabama Daughters of the American Revolution.
AlSAr	Alabama Department of Archives and History, Montgomery.
ALPLI	Allen County Public Library, Fort Wayne, Indiana.
AmRC	Amistad Research Center, New Orleans, Louisiana.
AzHS	Arizona Pioneers Historical Society, Tucson.
AzMBL	Arizona Mesa Branch Genealogical Library, Mesa.
BeHLUM	Bentley Historical Library, University of Michigan, Ann Arbor.
BoU	Boston University, Massachusetts.
BrHCDPL	Burton Historical Collection, Detroit Public Library, Michigan.
BriYU	Brigham Young University, Provo, Utah.
CaAr	California State Archives, Sacramento.
CaSL	California State Library, Sacramento.
CaSlSu	California State Library, Sutra.
ChHS	Chicago Historical Society, Illinois.
CnHS	Connecticut Historical Society, Hartford.
CnSL	Connecticut State Library, Hartford.
CoU	Colorado University, Boulder.
DAR	Daughters of the American Revolution, Washington, D.C.
DCoPL	Denver Public Library, Colorado.

DelHS	Delaware Historical Society, Wilmington.
DelPAr	Delaware Public Archives, Dover.
DuU	Duke University, Durham, North Carolina.
EaTU	East Tennessee State University, Johnson City.
FARC	Federal Archives and Records Center.
FilCK	Filson Club, Louisville, Kentucky.
FlSU	Florida State University, Tallahassee.
GasAR	Georgia State Department of Archives and History, Atlanta.
GaU	Georgia University, Athens.
GbSC	Glassboro State College, New Jersey
GLLDS	Genealogical Library, Church of Jesus Christ Latter-Day Saints.
GrHM	Greensboro Historical Museum, North Carolina.
HLSMCa	Henry Huntington Library, San Marino, California.
IaHS	Iowa Historical Society, Iowa City.
IaU	Iowa University, Iowa City.
IdSHS	Idaho State Historical Society, Boise.
IlHS	Illinois State Historical Society, Springfield.
IlSAr	Illinois State Archives, Springfield.
IndHS	Indiana Historical Society, Indianapolis.
IndSL	Indiana State Library, Indianapolis.
KaSHS	Kansas State Historical Society, Topeka.
KeHS	Kentucky Historical Society, Frankfort.
KeSCF	Kentucky State College, Frankfort.

LaSL Louisiana State Library, Baton Rouge.

LaU Louisiana State University, Baton Rouge.

LVPL Las Vegas Public Library, Nevada.

MaSAr Massachusetts Secretary of State. Archives Division, Boston.

MaUA Massachusetts University, Amherst.

MdSCPA Maryland State College, Princess Ann.

MeHS Maine Historical Society, Portland.

MeVS Maine Office of Vital Statistics, Augusta.

MilPL Milwaukee Public Library, Wisconsin.

MiSL Michigan State Library, Lansing.

MiU Michigan University, Ann Arbor.

MnHS Minnesota Historical Society, St. Paul.

MnSAr Minnesota State Archives, St. Paul.

MoHS Missouri Historical Society, St. Louis.

MoSHS Missouri State Historical Society, Columbia.

MoSL Missouri State Library, Jefferson City

MsDAR Mississippi Daughters of the American Revolution.

MsSAr Mississippi Department of Archives and History, Jackson.

MsU Mississippi University, University.

MtHS Montana Historical Society, Helena.

NAr National Archives and Records Service (US) Washington, D.C.

NCAr North Carolina Department of Archives and History, Raleigh.

NCU North Carolina University, Chapel Hill.

NDHS North Dakota Historical Society, Bismarck.

NeSHS Nebraska State Historical Society, Lincoln.

NHSL New Hampshire State Library, Concord.

NIaU Northern Iowa University, Cedar Rapids.

NJArRM New Jersey Archives and Records Management, Trenton.

NJBAr New Jersey State Library, Trenton.

NMU New Mexico University, Alberquerque.

NvSHS Nevada State Historical Society, Reno.

NvU Nevada University, Reno.

NYGBS New York Genealogical and Biographical Society, New York.

NYPL New York Public Library, New York.

NYScC New York Public Library, Schomburg Collection.

NYSL New York State Library, Albany.

OhSHS Ohio State Historical Society, Columbus.

OhU Ohio State University, Columbus.

OkHS Oklahoma Historical Society, Oklahoma City.

OrHS Oregon Historical Society, Portland.

OrSAr Oregon State Archives, Salem.

PeHS Historical Society of Pennsylvania, Philadelphia.

PeSL Pennsylvania State Library, Harrisburg.

PiU Pittsburgh University, Pennsylvania.

PrCo Providence College, Rhode Island.

RISL Rhode Island State Library, Providence.

RtSU Rutgers State University, New Brunswick, New Jersey.

SCHS	South Carolina Historical Society, Charleston.
SCSAr	South Carolina State Archives, Columbia.
SCU	South Carolina University, Columbia.
SDSHS	South Dakota State Historical Society, Pierre.
SoHCUNC	Southern Historical Collection, University of North Carolina, Chapel Hill.
SoMsU	Southern Mississippi University, Hattiesburg.
SpPL	Spokane Public Library, Washington.
StLPL	St. Louis Public Library, Missouri.
TeSL	Tennessee State Library and Archives, Nashville.
TxSL	Texas State Library, Austin.
ViSL	Virginia State Library, Richmond.
ViU	Virginia University, Charlottesville.
VtSL	Vermont State Library, Montpelier.
VtU	Vermont University and State College, Burlington.
WaSHS	Washington State Historical Society, Tacoma.
WaSL	Washington State Library, Olympia.
WinC	Winthrop College, Rock Hill, South Carolina.
WiSHS	Wisconsin State Historical Society, Madison.
WiU	Wisconsin University, Madison.
WPA	Works Projects Administration (United States).
WRHSC	Western Reserve Historical Society, Cleveland.
WVAr	West Virginia Department of Archives and History, Charleston.
WyAr	Wyoming State Archives and History Department, Cheyenne.